INTRACOASTAL WATERWAY

Restaurant Guide & Recipe Book

Authored by

Charles & Susan Eanes

"A Culinary Cruise Down The ICW"

ACKNOWLEDGEMENTS

Editorial copy, photography and design
by Charles Eanes

Editing & Marketing
by Susan Eanes

Photographic Credits:
Ritz Camera Centers, Inc. for color processing
Pg. 6-Author's photo by William Struhs
Pg. 12-Portsmouth Convention & Visitors Bureau
Pg. 25-North Carolina Division of Tourism
Pg. 34-Tom Doe
Pg. 62-Charleston Convention & Visitors Bureau
Pg. 66-William Struhs
Pg. 98-Amelia Now Magazine
Pg. 114-Kim Sargent & Cary Hazelgrove
Pg. 136-Van Woods, City of Miami

Library of Congress
Catalog Card Number: 98-073001

Published by Espichel Enterprises
First Edition Printed in the USA by
Carter Printing Co. Richmond, Virginia

Map Designs by:
Gerstenmaier Design Studios
Richmond, Virginia.

Visit our Website at www.dineashore.com
or on the ICW-Net at http://www.icw-net.com

U. S. Distributors:
Cruising Guide Publications
P.O. Box 1017
Dunedin, FL. 34697-1017
1-800-330-9542

Douglas Charles Press (Booksellers)
7 Adamsdale Road
North Attleboro, MA. 02760
(508) 761-7721 or 761-5414

Mailing Services, Inc. (Direct Wholesale Only)
P.O. Box 27486
Richmond, VA. 23261
(804) 359-2788

Robert Hale & Co. (Maritime Distributor)
1803 132th Ave. N.E. Suite #4
Bellvue, Wash. 98005
1-800-733-5330

RESTAURANT INFORMATION

SELECTION CRITERIA:

The restaurants selected for inclusion by the authors had to meet the following criteria:
They had to be within a reasonable distance of the Intracoastal Waterway and its tributaries or provide courtesy transportation for dining patrons.
The menus had to be varied and the quality of the cuisine consistently outstanding.
The staff and management had to be courteous, knowledgeable and offer excellent service.
The decor had to be attractive, clean, and provide a vista or congenial ambiance.
The wine list had to have depth and balance to complement the cuisine.

RESTAURANT DINING COSTS:

The dollar amounts shown for each restaurant indicate the starting price for breakfast and lunch and the main course for dinner, except where fixed dinner prices are noted. Dining costs, menus and restaurant hours change. Always call ahead for information.

CREDIT CARDS ACCEPTED:

AE=American Express VISA=VISA MC=Master Charge DISC=Discover DC=Diners Club

KEY TO SYMBOLS:

Reservations Accepted ....
Full Bar...................................
View ....
Romantic ....
Elegant ....
Casual...................................

Outdoor Dining...........................
Entertainment............................
Courtesy Transportation.............
Marina Facilities.........................
Boat or Dinghy Access...............
Wheelchair Access....................

CONTENTS

INTRODUCTION

THE AUTHORS, Susan & Charles Eanes, while sailing the Caribbean and the U.S. East Coast for the past 10 years, published four guides to the best restaurants and recipes found on Chesapeake Bay and every island from Puerto Rico to Antigua. Their books are filled with color photographs, stories and information on literally hundreds of restaurants with recipes from each chef, from barefoot bistros on remote islands to elegant five star resorts in major seaport cities. Originally intended as dining guides for fellow sailors these books have become classics for both the gourmand and cooks who enjoy the varied cuisines and recipes of some of the world's best professional chefs. The Eanes sailed 1200 miles along the Intracoastal Waterway and dined in over 200 restaurants to publish this latest issue of the very best found from Virginia, North Carolina, South Carolina, Georgia and Florida to the Keys.

THE INTRACOASTAL WATERWAY can be found running the entire length of the Nation's East Coast, but only from Mile Marker zero in the Elizabeth River between Norfolk and Portsmouth, Virginia does it flow continously through five Atlantic Coast states to end in the Florida Keys. This series of swamps, rivers and canals is known to boaters as the ICW or more affectionately, "The Ditch", but it is a safe inside passage when the outside Atlantic Ocean kicks up. Miles of no-wake zones and hundreds of bridges can slow traveling, but the scenery through small towns and skyscraper cities lining the banks, along with its cultural and culinary variety, makes cruising this aquatic Route 66 an incredible adventure. The Intracoastal Waterway offers choices of quiet anchorages where porpoise play, or modern marinas, resorts and restaurants where sailors play. Bon Voyage and Bon Appetit!

THE RESTAURANTS included in this guidebook were visited by the authors an average of six times to select the very best from the hundreds lining the Intracoastal Waterway and its tributaries. Each had to provide outstanding cuisine in a pleasant setting with courteous service and be located within a short walk or 10 minute ride from the waterfront or provide courtesy transportation for dining patrons. They vary from open air cafes for picking crabs on picnic tables to elegant world class dining rooms with linen, silverware and sommeliers. Those selected offer a diversity of ambiance, menus and cost that satisfies most every taste and purse. The symbols, stories and photographs allow you to make an accurate dining choice while avoiding overrated tourist traps and food factories. The restaurateurs featured are always anxious to please and if you visit with this book, your welcome will be a little extra special.

THE RECIPES provided by each restaurateur offer talented cooks an incredible variety of dishes from some of the best chefs on the East Coast as well as seafood recipes handed down through generations of watermen. Naturally seafood, fish, shellfish and crustaceans are featured in most restaurants that border the ICW, but you will also find exceptional recipes for venison, roast duck and wild game as well as rack of lamb, Chateaubriand and steak au poivre. For crab lovers there are dozens of choices from crab cakes to steamed, fried, baked, stuffed, deviled or sauteed soft shells. The recipes are concise though perhaps not for the novice cook and the photographs show how they are presented by each restaurant. Most of the ingredients can be found in supermarkets or gourmet specialty shops so you may now re-create your favorite restaurant dish at home for family and friends. Bon Appetit!!

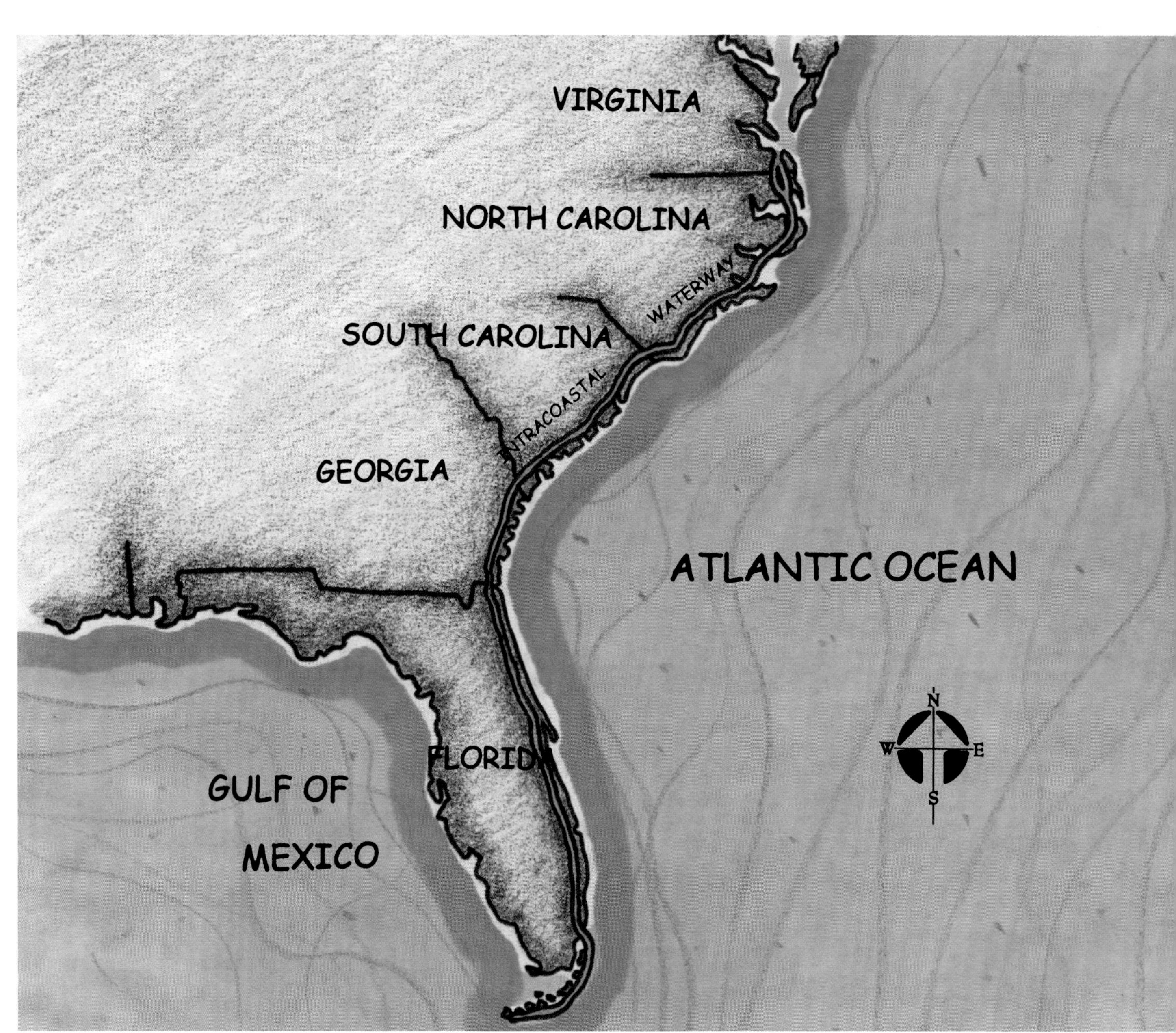
VIRGINIA
NORTH CAROLINA
SOUTH CAROLINA
WATERWAY
INTRACOASTAL
GEORGIA
ATLANTIC OCEAN
FLORIDA
GULF OF
MEXICO
N
W
E
S

INTRACOASTAL WATERWAY

The Atlantic Intracoastal Waterway is a unique collection of rivers, sounds, bays and creeks, all connected by man made canals that hug the coastline from New England to the Florida Keys. According to the U. S. Army Corps of Engineers, who maintain this aquatic highway, it officially begins at red buoy 36 in the Elizabeth River between Portsmouth and Norfolk, Virginia and flows through five States to tropical waters in the Florida Keys. Posted mile markers measure its serpentine course in statue miles as it meanders through swamps and coastal towns to major cities with skyscrapers lining it banks. The ICW offers a safe haven for vessels cruising the Southeast Coast and slices through a remarkable variety of landscapes, lifestyles, history and cuisines. By boat, or traveling adjacent roads, the Intracoastal Waterway is a fascinating passage of Americana!

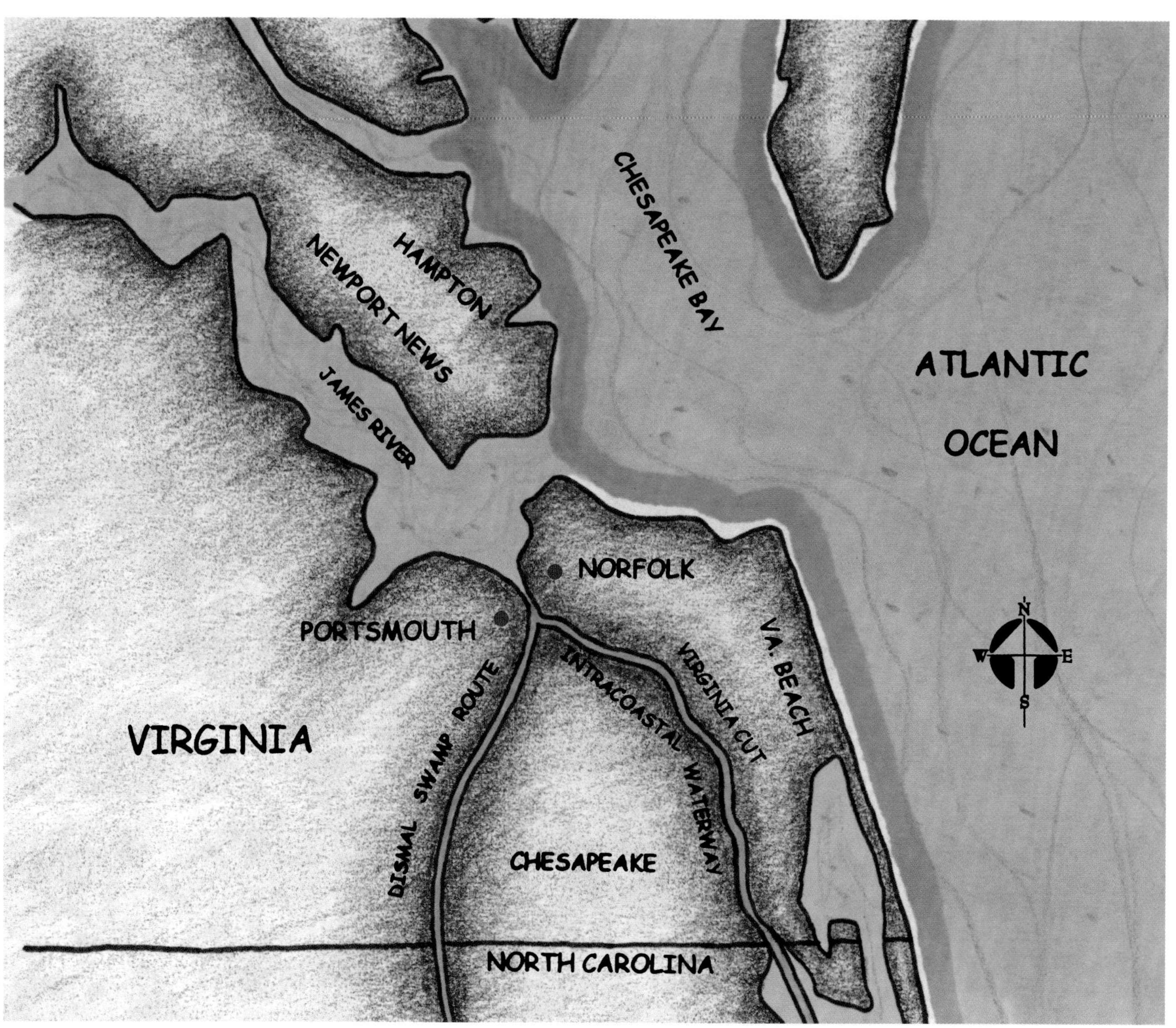
CHESAPEAKE BAY
HAMPTON
NEWPORT NEWS
JAMES RIVER
ATLANTIC
OCEAN
NORFOLK
PORTSMOUTH
VA. BEACH
N
W
E
S
INTRACOASTAL
VIRGINIA CUT
DISMAL SWAMP ROUTE
VIRGINIA
WATERWAY
CHESAPEAKE
NORTH CAROLINA

VIRGINIA *mm 0 to mm 34*

Virginia has thousands of miles of shoreline that front the Chesapeake Bay and its tributaries, but officially the Intracoastal Waterway does not start until one passes the Lighted Buoy "36" in the Elizabeth River just off Hospital Point between Portsmouth and Norfolk. In these port cities one will find all manner of restaurants featuring fresh Bay seafood and traditional Virginia recipes that date back to the days when sailing ships filled the harbor. It is still an ideal port of call for provisions and hungry sailors preparing for ocean voyages or for the private yatchsmen heading for warmer climes south on the ICW. At mile seven, boaters may elect to cruise to Albemarle Sound by way of the Virginia Cut or motor through the Great Dismal Swamp Canal and enjoy the natural beauty of its Wildlife Refuge. Either route offers hours of scenic wonders far removed from giant ships in a busy harbor, but also from the culinary delights found in these exceptional restaurants.

Portsmouth *mm 0*

It is fitting that Portsmouth, a city with over 300 years of maritime history, should mark the official entrance to the Intracoastal Waterway at Mile Marker Zero. As one of the oldest working harbors in the country, it is home today to the nation's largest naval shipyard and the Tidewater Yacht Marina, a 325 deep water slip, full service marina. The city has one of the largest collections of antique homes in Virginia where walking tours of Olde Towne retrace American history from Revolutionary times to World War II. While preserving its character for generations, Portsmouth also offers visitors modern day attractions in their Children's, Naval Shipyard and Art museums, antique shops, art galleries and some of the finest restaurants on the ICW waterfront. The City of Portsmouth hosts a series of social and boating events year around. For the full story call 1* 800 * PORTS * VA.

AMORY'S WHARF

Tidewater Yacht Marina 10 Crawford Parkway (757) 399-0991
Lunch $7 Dinner $15 Closed Mon. Lunch

At mile post zero, one could not hope to find a better culinary start or ending to a trip on the ICW than this restaurant in the Tidewater Yacht Marina at Portsmouth. From a family famous as fresh seafood suppliers, chef David Amory is still an avid fisherman but now his catches become delicious appetizers and entrees. Their menu will feature 8 fresh fish daily, seasoned to perfection, steamed, pan fried or broiled or sauteed in olive oil like his scallops and oysters finished with spinach, bacon, cream and cheeses. A graduate of CIA, David is renowned for his she crab soup, oysters Rockefeller and a pan seared lobster and beef special served in natural juices with mushrooms, herbs and a bit of sherry. He combines soft shell crabs and a grilled pork loin with a balsamic vinaigrette as his special "Chesapeake Tradition" to satisfy both seafood and meat lovers. Amory's view of the busy ICW waterway is spectacular, but it is David's exceptional talent as a chef that keeps the Wharf packed. With his wife LeAnn they cater private parties or offer take outs, but always ask for hush puppies....they are worth the trip alone!

Blackened Scallops & Lobster with Lobster Sauce

2 1-1/2 lbs lobsters
1 lb scallops
1-1/2 pt whipping cream
2 tblsp each, finely chopped parsley, basil, mushrooms & tomato
blackening season
black & red caviar

Simmer whole lobsters in cream for 12 mins covered. Remove tail meat, return lobster bodies to cream & simmer 1 hour uncovered. Cut tail meat into chunks & set aside. Coat one side of scallops with blackening season & sear in hot dry pan. Remove shells from sauce, add lobster chunks, mushrooms & tomato, salt & pepper to taste & reheat. Pour sauce on plates, arrange scallops & garnish with red & black caviar, basil & parsley. Serves 4.

COCK ISLAND GRILL

Holiday Inn 8 Crawford Parkway (757) 393-2573 Major Credit Cards
Brkfst $5 Lunch $8 Dinner $15

Its location in the historic Olde Towne section of Portsmouth with a panoramic view of the Elizabeth River and Norfolk's skyline make Cock Island Grill one of Holiday Inns' most unique restaurants. Add to this both contemporary and traditional cuisine by chef Joseph Landon and you can understand why it is a favorite of both locals and yachtsmen on the ICW. Using old family recipes dating back to 1702, Joe prepares plantation style meals from catfish and eggs for breakfast to gourmet treats of oysters and ham. For an island flair they offer Mahi Mahi with pineapple salsa, a spicy Thai pasta with shrimp or conch fritters and jerk chicken. Crawfish, clams and crab are steamed or prepared with steak, pork or chicken for delectable dinners as well as BBQ ribs and a prime rib of beef served nightly. Its name derives from history when cock fights were held on these shores where today patrons enjoy watching boat races and huge ships as they dine and dance to live music. The Holiday Inn caters business or social functions and offers a great escape for boaters and visitors looking for a relaxing and delicious dining experience ashore.

Grilled Mahi Mahi w/ Pineapple Relish

4 8 oz cuts of Mahi Mahi
3/4 cup white vinegar
1/2 cup oil
1 cup pineapple juice
pinch of pepper
1 sprig chopped fresh dill

Marinate Mahi Mahi in next 5 ingredients for 2 hours. Remove & grill on open flame 3 mins on each side. To make relish: Combine 1/2 cup each of pineapple juice, vinegar & sugar & bring to a boil. Thicken with 1 tblsp corn starch. Pour mixture over 1/2 cup each of diced red, green & yellow peppers & 1 cup each of diced pineapple & chopped mango. Cover 30 mins & chill. Arrange Mahi Mahi on plate & spoon relish over. Serve with grilled vegetable medley. Serves four.

BRUTTI'S

467 Dinwiddie Street, Old Towne (757) 393-1923 Major Credit Cards
Brkfst $4 Lunch $5

You might say that Charles Greenhood's magical touch with food comes from his being the grandson of a grocer and son of a caterer. Or it may come from living in the French West Indies for years, but whatever the reason Brutti's Bistro creates some of the best breakfast and lunch dishes found in Old Towne. He started with an eight seat espresso bar serving Parisian style sandwiches on freshly baked baguettes that became so popular he expanded and added sidewalk dining as well. His menu, too, has grown but his Mandarin, Lemon Pepper and Cashew Chicken are still served on hot French baguettes along with turkey, tuna, beef and pastrami and a variety of cheese and sauces. Brutti's is also famous for their huge Greek salad and a French Brie Mandorle that are works of art. Home baked pastries and croissants, cheese filled "bagel nuts", fresh coffee of every style and flavor and a huge Weekend Brunch, plus catering and take outs, keep Charles and his wife, Kathy, busy with plans for larger quarters with dinner service, soon. Brutti's just won both the Peoples Choice and Judges Award for "Taste of Portsmouth 1998"!

Brutti's French Brie Mandorle

2 4 oz wedges French brie
2 oz slivered almonds
2 tblsps honey
1/2 fresh cantaloupe
1/2 fresh honey dew melon
4 oz fresh grapes
3 large fresh strawberries

Coat brie wedges with honey and heat for 20 to 30 seconds in microwave oven or until it begins to run. Meanwhile cut melon and cantaloupe into thin half moon slices. Place melted brie in center of plates and sprinkle with slivered almonds. Arrange slices of melon and canteloupe around brie on three sides. Cut strawberries in half and arrange over sliced fruit. Add grapes and serve with sliced French baguette. Serves two.

THUMPERS

Corner of County & Court Streets (757) 399-1024 AE VISA MC
Lunch $6 Dinner $9

No one is sure of how Thumpers got its name, but there are striking similarities between a huge imposing paper mache rabbit and the restaurant's owner Robert Conery. Both wear sandals, impish grins and slight paunch, suggesting they know what good food and good times are all about and everyone who has wined and dined here know this to be a fact. Their menu which runs from lunch and dinner to late night snacks offers everything from fried gater or Cajun jambalaya to shrimp remoulade or Caribbean chicken. There are 13 appetizers to chose from, a dozen sandwiches and burgers, all with Boars Head meats served with cross cut potato fries as well as steamed oysters, crabs, clams or veggies. You can have a N.Y. strip, filet mignon or Greek pizza all for around $10 or enjoy one of their nightly specials with part of your proceeds going to a local charity. There is live entertainment weekly and upstairs the bar and billiards room rocks to the wee hours. Only a few blocks from the waterfront, Thumpers is a lively addition to this old historic section of Portsmouth. For sailor or landlubber, it's a great "Port of Call"!

Thumper's Catfish Stuffed with Crab

4 6 oz catfish fillets
1/2 lb crab meat
1 small red pepper
1 small green pepper
2 green onions
2 tblsps mayonnaise
1 tsp Old Bay
1/4 cup bread crumbs
salt & pepper
butter

Finely chop red & green peppers & onions & mix with mayonnaise, Old Bay seasoning & bread crumbs. Add crab meat & mix lightly. Cut pocket in catfish fillets & fill with mound of crab mixture. Brush fillets with melted butter, season with salt & pepper & bake in 350 degree oven until fillets are done & crab mix is brown. Serve with black beans, rice & tomato salsa & garlic toast. Serves four.

COMMODORE THEATRE

421 High Street (757) 393-6962 2 Shows Nightly, Matinee Wed-Sat-Sun
Lunch $6 Dinner $11 Major Credit Cards

This will be one of the most entertaining meals you could ever find on the ICW, for you dine in a beautifully restored art deco theatre facing a huge movie screen with Dolby Digital sound that puts you in the middle of the latest Hollywood releases. The new Commodore Theatre is the creation of Fred Schoenfeld, who began in show business with Norman Powell 30 years ago. Fred's Theatre fills with movie lovers in comfortable swivel chairs while enjoying a delightful matinee or evening meal. Their menu "Previews" showcase appetizers from popcorn and onion rings to chicken drummettes or spicy potato wedges. "Feature Presentations" include salads, fruit and cheese plates, pizza, fantail shrimp and sandwiches made with Boar's Head meats. They are famous for homemade chicken salad with almonds, raisins and celery, as well as some "Great Endings" like hot deep dish apple pie, Tiramisu, or freshly baked cinnamon loaf. Fred's Theatre is available for private shows, but for a rare entertaining experience just visit the Commodore to enjoy a movie, and dine with the Stars!!

The Commodore's Chicken Salad

2 lbs chicken breasts, skinned & boneless
1/2 cup pineapple juice
1/2 cup soy sauce
1 tblsp ginger powder
1/4 cup vanilla extract
3/4 cup cooking oil
2 cups mayonnaise
1 cup sour cream
1/2 cup mandarin oranges
1/2 tblsp dill weed
1/2 tblsp celery seed
juice of 1/2 lemon
1 med celery stalk, sliced
1/2 cup white raisins
1/3 cup slivered almonds

Marinate chicken in mixture of next five ingredients for 24 hours. Grill chicken until done, cool & cut into small cubes. Combine cubes with next 6 ingredients. Add last 3 ingredients & toss lightly. Mound chicken salad on plate or on a roll & serve with fresh fruit. Serves 6.

Norfolk *mm 0*

Hampton Roads has been a major port of call for ships from around the world from the earliest days of sailing vessels to the huge ocean liners of today. As a part of the second largest harbor on the East Coast, Norfolk's waterfront is lined with piers and docks for tankers, colliers, cruise ships and containerships as well as submarines, aircraft carriers and warships that make up the largest U.S. Naval base in the world. Norfolk's downtown Waterside Marina has also become a favorite destination for private yachts who tie up to enjoy shopping and dining and provisioning at the headwaters of the Intracoastal Waterway. For yachtsmen cruising the ICW, it is perhaps the first or last major port along the Southeastern coast until reaching Charleston or Savannah. The city as a major financial center has also attracted more sophisticated restaurateurs who offer a variety of dining choices. The following selection is among the best within a short distance of the waterfront.

MAUDE'S HOUSE

313 West Bute Street (757) 622-4990 Closed Sundays
Lunch $5 Dinner $12 VISA MC

This former 19th century carriage house with its cobblestone courtyard has been transformed into a bright, intimate little restaurant with white brick walls splashed with brilliant colors in paintings and buckets of fresh flowers. Just as colorful and bright is its founder, Heather Whitehead, an Australian former pharmacist whose alchemy in the kitchen packed Maude's House for lunch and dinner. The chalkboard menu changes daily with lots of fresh fish and pastas and superb sauces and vegetables. It is famous for tomato pie appetizers, a chicken liver pate, charred tuna or their crawfish and tomato cream sauce over penne pasta. Lunches are delicious diversions with buffalo burgers, veggie grilled sandwiches or superb roasted eggplant. This "down under" dynamo cafe always features a chargrilled Australian rack of lamb served with a fresh mint sauce that is incomparable. Maude's House is still fondly called an "Australian oasis in Norfolk" even though the new owner, Omar Boukhriss hails from Morocco. He still flys the Aussie flag out front and Heather's cuisine flys from the kitchen!

Rockfish with Rum Pepper Glaze & Mango Coulis

4 6 oz rockfish fillets
3/4 cup rum
4 tblsps roasted & ground oriental peppercorns
zest & juice of 2 limes
1/4 cup soy sauce
1/2 cup sugar

Combine rum, peppercorns, lime zest & juice, sugar & soy sauce & reduce over low heat to a thick glaze. Spread glaze over rockfish fillets & pan sear on one side. Place in 350 degree oven for 8 minutes or until desired doneness. To make coulis: Combine & blend until smooth 3 tblsps orange juice, 3 tblsps dry white wine, 1-1/2 cups of mango, peeled & cubed & 1/2 diced chipotle pepper. Drizzle over rockfish & garnish with mango & tomato salsa. Serves 4.

WILD MONKEY

1603 Colley Ave. (757) 627-6462 AE VISA MC
Lunch $6 Dinner $11 Closed Sat. Lunch & Sundays

This is one wild no nonsense in your face place that says out front "No high chairs, no reservations, no pink wine and no carry-outs", but if you want some really, really good eating it is more than worth an occasional wait just to dine here. There is also no printed menu, for one wall is a giant chalkboard with over forty constantly changing regional items listing the latest eclectic creations of chef Peter Pittman. Things like grilled lamb and mashed potatoes, Smithfield pork chops, garlic mussels, and abundance of local fish and seafood and it's "home of the Ten Dollar Meatloaf." Sandwiches are piled high on fresh baked breads and all the basic foodstuffs are prepared in house and served in large portions. The wine list covers the entire other wall with the actual bottles displayed and brief tasting notes for each. Wild Monkey is repeatedly selected as one of Norfolk's best dining experiences and wins awards for its innovative wine listing as well. This popular Ghent bistro is perhaps best described as hip, chick and Bohemian, where patrons have "Gone Bananas" for Peter's casual, but very serious cuisine!

Wild Monkey Pork Chops with Honey Wine Sauce

4 6 oz bone in, center cut pork chops
2 oz butter
2/3 cup Cabernet red wine
1/3 cup honey
kosher salt
fresh cracked black pepper

Season both sides of pork chops with kosher salt & cracked black pepper two hours ahead. Sear one side of chops in butter in hot saute pan. Flip chops over & finish cooking in 400 degree oven 5 to 6 minutes or until desired doneness. Remove chops & deglaze pan with red wine. Add honey & reduce to bubbly syrup. Place chops over mashed potatoes & drizzle sauce over. Serve with steamed vegetables & garnish with rosemary & sage sprigs. Serves two.

MAGNOLIA STEAK

749 W. Princess Anne Rd. (757) 625-0400 Closed for lunch Sat & Sun
Lunch $6 Dinner $12 AE VISA MC

Magnolia is known to locals as the most serious steak house in Norfolk. Here they use only Angus beef, cut and aged to exacting standards and cooked in special 1800 degree ovens to precise diner's taste, from a sirloin or filet mignon to a cowboy-size Kansas City strip or a 40 oz porterhouse for two. But steak is only one of the many culinary treasures you will discover here. Their menu changes with the seasons to offer the freshest in salads, vegetables, seafood and pasta choices, all served in large portions with freshly baked breads.

Evening specials feature a variety of oyster dishes and include a fresh catch of the day from red snapper, swordfish or tuna to salmon and flounder. As owners, chef and maitre'd, Tracey and David Holmes have made Magnolia one of those rare finds where guests are treated as their personal friends. They will even send their limo to bring you from the marina or town hotel. After dinner they offer single malt scotch or port and cigars in the bar and pool room which hops until 2:00 am. Magnolia is one fabulous steak house that has something for everyone!

Cowboy Steak with Orzo Custard

4 16 oz bone-in ribeyes
1 lb orzo pasta
1 cup beef stock
3 cups half & half cream
8 oz cream cheese
4 oz feta cheese, crumbled
2 eggs, lightly beaten
1/2 cup chopped parsley
1 cup tasso ham, diced fine
fresh pepper to taste

Cook orzo pasta in salted water, al dente. Drain & rinse with cool water. Combine beef stock with cream cheese over low heat to melt cheese. Stir in last ingredients & mix well. Add cooked orzo & stir. Place mixture in 13 x9x2" greased baking dish and cook in 350 degree preheated oven for 25 minutes until set. Mound custard on plate and top with ribeye steak grilled to your liking. Serves four.

BIENVILLE GRILL

723 W. 21st St. (757) 625-5427 Closed Mondays & for Lunch Sat. & Sun.
Lunch $7 Dinner $13 Major Credit Cards

Owner Mike Hall greets his patrons with "Where Y'At", a Louisiana expression meaning "How are you?". Mike spent 12 years cooking in New Orleans after training in Paris for his certified chef degree from Cordon Bleu. His menu now features the best of both worlds from Cajun to classic American cuisine with French flavors. Crawfish & Corn Maque Choux, Chicken Papillote with smoked salmon and shrimp roasted in parchment, grilled catfish over jambalaya or bronzed scallops with a meuniere sauce typify his creativity. His New York strips and pork tenderloins are fire grilled and served over fettucini, mashers or rice with a smoked tomato corn or blackened voodo sauce. Salads include Bienville Caesar or Nicoise, pepper seared tuna over mixed greens or a roasted vegetable coulis over pasta. Happy hour specials almost every day, a weekly crawfish boil, and live music on weekends keeps the Bienville Grill as delicious and lively as a Mardi Gras. It's in the historic Ghent section of Norfolk, only a short taxi ride from Waterside, but if you get lost just call Mike and say "Where Y'At"!

Bienville Grill Chicken Big Easy

4 6 oz boneless chicken breasts
Cajun seasoning
6 oz Andouille sausage
6 oz crawfish tails
1 tblsp chopped green onion
1 tblsp butter
2 cups heavy cream or thin Bechamel sauce
salt & pepper

Sprinkle chicken breasts with cajun seasoning, lightly brush with oil & grill until done. To make Big Easy sauce, saute diced Andouille sausage, crawfish & green onion in butter. Add cream & reduce 25% or add Bechamel sauce. Salt & pepper to taste. Arrange chicken breasts on mashed potatoes & serve with Big Easy sauce & sauteed vegetable medley. Serves 4.

CAFE 21

742-G West 21st Street (757) 625-4218 Major Credit Cards
Lunch $7 Dinner $13 Closed Tuesdays

It's always a pleasant surprise to discover a restaurant that is both casual and chic, almost hidden among grocery and drug stores in a mini mall. Yet that is certainly the case with Cafe 21, where the decor and cuisine are as sophisticated as one might find on Park Avenue, but at half the price. Proprietress Diane Fentress has an American Mediterranean menu that is a refreshing reprieve from the mundane. While retaining Cafe Classics like Isabelle's down home meatloaf, baby back ribs and other patron favorites, they create delicious new specialties weekly.

Consider mussels roasted with garlic, tomato and saffron or feta cheese and greens with a lemon oregano vinaigrette as starters, followed with seared salmon, horseradish potato cakes and wilted spinach as an entree. Or try their grilled doublecut pork chop and wild mushroom risotto or even one of their designer pizzas stuffed with chicken, sausage or shrimp and roasted red peppers. It is wise to check their showcase of desserts on entering, for it is your visual clue to a sumptuous lunch or dinner you are sure to enjoy at Diane's rejuvenated Cafe 21.

Salmon w/ Potato Cakes & Spinach

2 7 oz salmon steaks
1/2 lb fresh spinach
1/2 lb russet potatoes
1 tblsp horseradish
1 large red pepper
1 medium onion
2 tblsps white wine
cornstarch, olive oil, butter

Season salmon with salt & pepper & sear in very hot olive oil. Meanwhile saute spinach in olive oil & white wine until wilted. Add roasted & julienned red pepper. Boil potatoes & mash with buttermilk & butter. Cool & add horseradish, chopped spinach & caramelized onion. Make patties,dust with cornstarch & cook on griddle till brown. Place salmon over potato cakes & spinach. Garnish with red pepper coulis & sour cream with lime juice. Serves two.

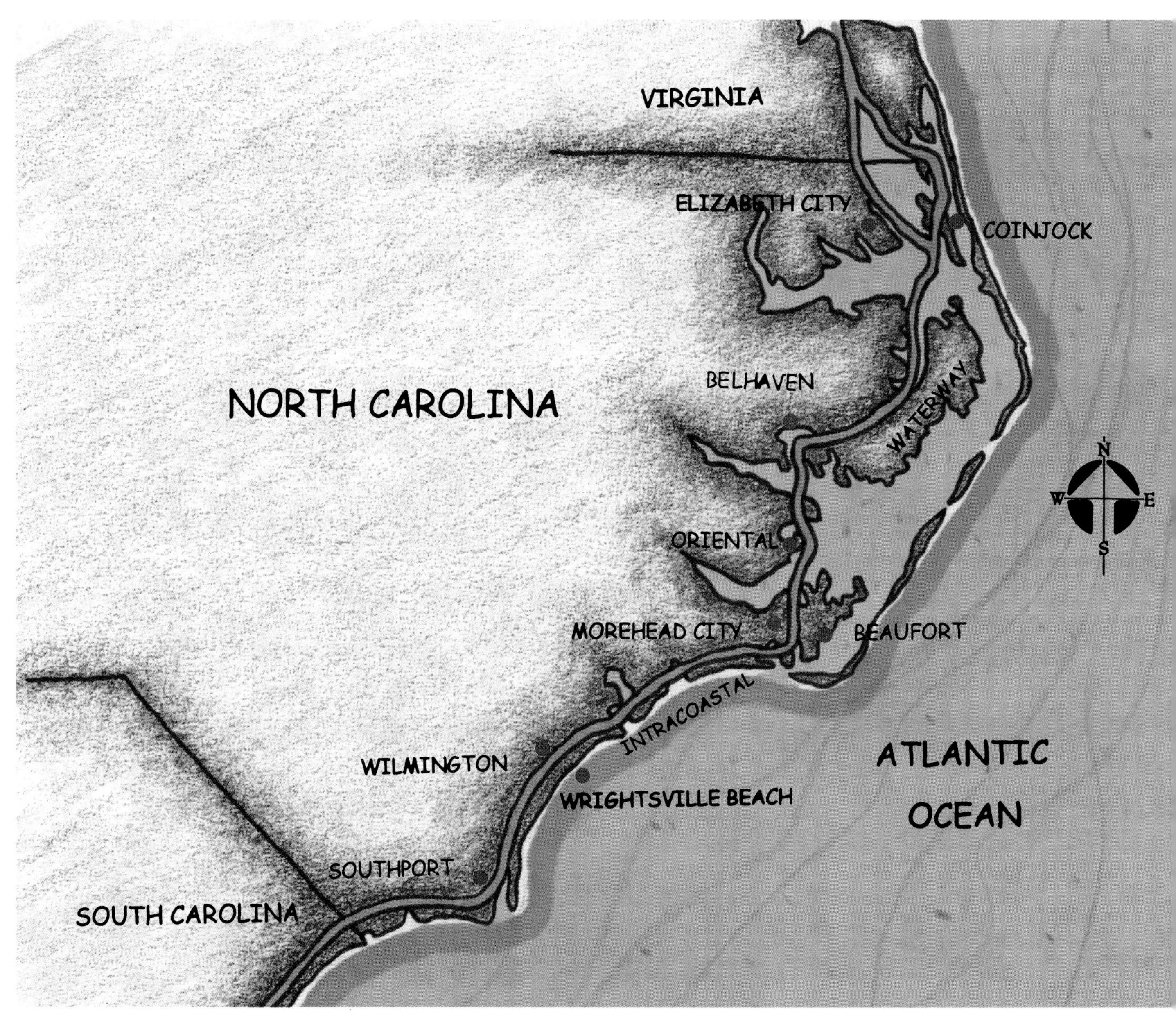
VIRGINIA
ELIZABETH CITY
COINJOCK
BELHAVEN
NORTH CAROLINA
WATERWAY
N
W
E
S
ORIENTAL
MOREHEAD CITY
BEAUFORT
INTRACOASTAL
ATLANTIC
OCEAN
WILMINGTON
WRIGHTSVILLE BEACH
SOUTHPORT
SOUTH CAROLINA

NORTH CAROLINA *mm 34 to 342*

There are few coastal states that offer scenery as varied as you will discover traveling along the Intracoastal Waterway through North Carolina. The remote but beautiful Dismal Swamp, wide beaches, dunes and marshes along the famous Outer Banks and Cape Hatteras and the inland rivers and sounds extending to Southport and Cape Fear provide interesting side trips from the ICW. The waterfront towns like Elizabeth City, Belhaven, Oriental, Beaufort, Morehead City, Wilmington and Wrightsville Beach are lined with historic sites, shops, marinas and restaurants that welcome boaters and land travelers alike. About the only consistency you find along this coastline is the friendliness of North Carolinians and the excellence of the cuisine from good ol' Southern cooking and fresh local seafood to outstanding gourmet dishes found in the following restaurants.

Elizabeth City mm 51

For those cruising down the naturally beautiful but remote Dismal Swamp, Elizabeth City will be a welcome change of pace offering all the conveniences a modern town provides. You will also discover it is one of the friendliest receptions you will encounter on the entire Intracoastal Waterway. The city offers free dockage on the waterfront and visitors are met with personal greetings, rose buds for each lady crewmember and a neat welcome package from the volunteer "Rose Buddies". In easy walking distance are blocks of historic old homes, shops, bakeries, cafes and restaurants to satisfy any taste or need for boaters or land travelers. History records adventurous English settlers were here long before Jamestown with visits from the pirate Blackbeard, Edgar Allen Poe and George Washington. One wonders if their reception and dining were nearly as warm and tasteful as found in Elizabeth City today!

MULLIGAN'S Waterfront Grille

400 Water Street (252) 331-2431 Major Credit Cards
Lunch $6 Dinner $11

What once housed a tractor dealership has been transformed into a beautiful waterfront mall with offices, gift shops, boutiques and an attractive restaurant providing open air decks and panoramic views of the Elizabeth City harbor. This new Water Works complex has helped revitalize the downtown waterfront with parks, tree lined walks and free slips for visiting boaters on the ICW. Mulligan's Grille has also stimulated the culinary community with menus featuring fresh local seafood as well as seasonal favorites of wild game or prime rib and steaks. You can order a catch of the day grilled, blackened, Provencale or Cajun style or select a daily special of Seafood Primavera, Maryland crab cakes or fresh oysters broiled with jalapeno, bacon and cheddar. In season the decks open for lunch and dinner, or catered social events with a Gazebo bar for weekly live entertainment. Known as the friendliest place on the ICW, where Rose Buddies present rose buds to visiting ladies, Elizabeth City and Mulligan's now offer a menu of tantalizing tastes to lure travelers along the beautiful Pasquotank River and ICW.

Mulligan's Seafood Pasta Primavera

16 large shrimp, cleaned
16 sea scallops
1/2 lb salmon fillets, cubed
2 cups fresh vegetables, sliced yellow & green squash, red onion, red & green peppers, broccoli & mushrooms
4 tblsps butter
2 minced garlic cloves
1 tblsp parsley, chopped
1 tblsp capers
1/4 cup dry white wine
4 portions linguine

Saute minced garlic, capers & parsley in butter & wine. Add shrimp, scallops & salmon & simmer until half cooked. Add vegetables & saute until tender crisp. Cook linguine al dente & divide onto 4 plates. Spoon seafood vegetable mix over pasta & garnish with lemon wedge & greens.
Serves four.

ARENA'S BAKERY & DELI

700 Main Street (252) 335-2114 Closed Sat Evening & Sunday
Bkfst $2 Lunch $4 Dinner $5 AE VISA MC

The aroma of freshly baked bread from this cozy corner deli is enough to entice any passerby to take a closer look. It is but one of the reasons this relatively new restaurant has been so successful since the day it opened, for inside you will find a cornucopia of breads and pastries, sandwiches and subs, soups and salads. It is all the handiwork of Michelle Arena who daily bakes 11 different breads from French baguettes to Italian foccacia which she sells by the loaf or for sandwiches piled high with Boar's Head meats and cheeses. Her bread also comes with 9 different salads, served in large portions with homemade dressings. This spotless deli is ideal for a breakfast of cream cheese danishes, bagels or croissants, scones and muffins with fresh roasted coffee or herbal tea. It is also the perfect place for boaters to resupply with gourmet meats, cheeses, bread, pastries, wines and beer. Arena creates a variety of sweets, cakes and pies from pecan to a sinful peanut butter. Her gift baskets called a Dinner for Two, Romantic Getaway or Ships Ahoy are all examples of Arena's culinary talents.

Arena's Peanut Butter Pie

2 cups peanut butter cookie crumbs
2 cups chocolate graham cookie crumbs
1 stick butter
3 cups whipping cream
24 oz soft cream cheese
2 cups peanut butter
1-1/2 cups sugar
2 tblsps vanilla

Combine cookie crumbs & butter & press into two 9" pie plates & freeze. Chill a bowl & beat whipping cream until stiff. In separate bowl mix cream cheese & sugar. Add peanut butter & vanilla & beat till smooth. Fold whipped cream into peanut butter mixture & spoon into pie crust. Top with chopped peanuts & refrigerate. Melt 1-1/2 cups chocolate chips with 4 tblsps heavy cream & drizzle over pies. Makes two pies.

THE SECRET ROOM

108 E. Fearing Street (252) 338-2177 Major Credit Cards
Dinner $14 Dinner Only Wed thru Sat

For years a huge shrub almost hid this 1847 building causing guests to name it The Secret Room. Today it is no secret that this room serves the finest gourmet dining found anywhere along this section of the ICW. Proprietors Joe and Darla Semonich have transformed this historic old lodge into an English style setting where sumptuous dinners are served along with homemade sour cream biscuits and delicious desserts. Darla changes the menu weekly as Joe uses only fresh foods and produce in all of his recipes. He is famous for his crab cakes, soft shells and a southern dish of grits with herbs, cheese, bacon and sauteed shrimp. Your choice of poultry, seafood, beef or nightly specials is served with fresh steamed vegetables, or his secret carrot souffle or a surprise Heavenly Honeydew salad. An adjoining courtyard, used for private catered groups, connects The Secret Room to the Elizabeth City Bed and Breakfast, their other historic landmark, offering rooms with antiques, wicker and comfortable beds. The Secret Room is the ideal gourmet hideaway for both boater or land traveler.

Secret Room Heavenly Honeydew Salad

4 egg yolks
1/4 cup cider vinegar
1 tblsp sugar
1 tblsp butter
1/2 tsp salt
dash of ground red pepper
12 large marshmallows
1/2 cup whipping cream

Combine first 6 ingredients & cook over medium heat while stirring until thick & smooth. Add marshmallows & stir until smooth. Cool & fold in whipped cream. Peel & slice 1/2 honeydew, 2 kiwi, 2 peaches, 1 cup raspberries & 1/2 large pineapple peeled & cut into chunks. Arrange fruit on bed of bibb lettuce & pour dressing over salad. Sprinkle with 1 cup walnut pieces. Serves four.

MARINA RESTAURANT

Camden Causeway by Pelican Marina (252) 335-7307 Closed Mon.
Lunch $6 Dinner $13 VISA MC

If ever there was a seafood restaurant that has passed the test of time and still packs them in after 27 years, it would certainly be the Marina Restaurant on the Camden Causeway in Elizabeth City. Owner Margie Basnight built a reputation for serving the freshest seafood available and now her son, Clarence, catches tuna, wahoo and mahi-mahi offshore that is hooked, cooked and served within hours. Daughter Vicky runs the kitchen and uses Margie's recipes to prepare Marina specials like their spicy clam chowder or scallops, crabmeat and shrimp panned in butter with wine and spices. Every item is fresh so soft shells, oysters and locally grown vegetables are seasonal. Early bird specials offer ham, seafood, chicken, liver or cutlets with two veggies for about $6 or you can enjoy prime rib or steaks cut to order. Their dining rooms, open decks and upstairs raw bar provide beautiful views of the harbor at sunset. Besides the great food and vistas, it is the friendliness of Margie's family and staff that has made Marina Restaurant a favorite of both locals and boaters for so many years.

Hatteras Clam Chowder

2 lbs diced clams w/ juice
1/4 lb bacon
4 onions
4 large potatoes
4 celery stalks
1 tblsp salt
1 tblsp pepper
1/4 bottle Texas Pete hot sauce

Cut bacon into small pieces & dice the onions, potatoes & celery stalks. Place all ingredients into large stock pot & add water to cover completely. Bring pot to a boil while stirring often. Reduce heat and simmer for 45 minutes testing potatoes for doneness. Cool & refrigerate for one day. Heat chowder as needed & serve with steamed shrimp topped with crabmeat & dry white wine. Makes one gallon.

COINJOCK MARINA RESTAURANT

Coinjock, N.C. (252) 453-3271 Seasonal openings for dinner
Dinner $11 VISA MC

Ask anyone who has traveled the entire Intracoastal Waterway where to find the best and biggest steaks and invariably their answer will be the Coinjock Marina Restaurant in North Carolina. They are famous for serving a giant size 32 ounce prime rib that is juicy, lean and roasted to perfection. Just as popular as those super size steaks is a variety of seafood dishes from grilled marinated tuna or mahi mahi to fresh oysters or soft shell crabs in season. They prepare the lightest, tastiest catfish and flounder you will ever find served with cole slaw, fresh vegetables and hushpuppies. And if you are looking for a perfect example of Southern hospitality, owners Jeanne, Carl and Louis Davis offer that in large measure as well. Even their wait staff serves large portions of friendliness along with a variety of fresh seafood, chicken, sizzling steaks and homemade desserts baked daily like chocolate chess or pecan pies. Coinjock Marina has one of the best prices on the ICW to fill your yacht with fuel and boat supplies as well as filling up your crew on huge steaks, seafood and lots of friendship.

Coinjock Flounder with Lump Crab

4 6 oz flounder fillets
8 oz lump crabmeat
butter
seafood seasoning
parsley for garnish

Lightly season flounder fillets on both side with seafood seasoning. Baste in butter and saute for several minutes or until two thirds done. Mound 4 ounces of pure crabmeat, with no filler, on each of two fillets and place other two fillets on top of each. Lightly sprinkle tops with seafood seasoning and place under broiler until lightly browned. Place fillets on plates and serve with steamed vegetables and hushpuppies and garnish with parsley. Serves two.

RIVER FOREST MANOR

738 East Main Street (252) 943-2151 MC VISA
Lunch $7 Dinner $16

For yachtsmen, the River Forest Manor in Belhaven is one of the most familiar and complete ports of call on the ICW. This turn of the century mansion offers every amenity from guest rooms filled with antiques, to tennis courts, pool, jacuzzi and a full service shipyard capable of repairing and overhauling vessels large or small. But perhaps the most memorable attraction is a world famous smorgasbord that is the epitome of southern manor house dining. It is an awesome display from salad bar to homemade ice creams and pies, buttermilk cheese biscuits and vegetables cooked country style, picked fresh from the Manor's gardens. There's crabmeat casserole, oyster fritters, ham, soft shell crabs, shrimp, baked fish, fried chicken or strip steaks cooked to order. Enjoying sumptuous cuisine in Victorian parlors under crystal chandeliers is a rare experience offered daily at River Forest Manor. Since 1947 this grand old estate has hosted celebrities from James Cagney to Walter Cronkite and today Melba Smith and sons Axson, Jr. and Mark continue their tradition that has served so many so well for 50 years.

River Forest Manor Crabmeat Casserole Appetizer

1 cup crabmeat
1 large red Bermuda onion
1 small green pepper
butter
croutons
1 tsp seafood seasoning

Cut 1/2 red Bermuda onion into very thin slices and chop into small pieces. Cut green pepper into thin small strips and saute with onion in butter until tender crisp. Add croutons, seafood seasoning and mix well. Shred crabmeat and stir into mixture of onions, peppers and croutons. Mound crabmeat casserole onto plate and garnish with very thin slices of red onion. Serves two.

THE TRAWL DOOR

Water Street, at the foot of Oriental Bridge (252) 249-1232
Lunch $6 Dinner $15 VISA MC DISC

Trawl doors are used to keep huge nets below the surface for sweeping up tons of shrimp and seafood. It is a most appropriate name for this restaurant that has swept up culinary awards for 20 years of excellence in its cuisine, service and ambiance. Jim and Lois Moye bought this old 1900's building that served Oriental as a hardware and grocery store, reopened it as The Trawl Door Restaurant and over the years made it into the largest and most popular dining spot on this section of the ICW. Their formula was simply "to get it right every night", using only fresh high quality foods, expertly prepared and served in a pleasant nautical atmosphere by a staff noted for friendliness. Any item you select, from a spicy red crab soup to prime rib, Maine lobster or one of many seafood specials, is bound to satisfy both palate and purse. There are rooms for intimate dining, family affairs with kid menus, large banquets and a bar room for watching sports while eating pizzas and baskets of finger foods. Aside from outstanding cuisine, The Trawl Door has a flavor of friendship that is hard to beat!

Seafood Mediterranean

8 oz scallops
8 oz shrimp
4 oz feta cheese
fettucini for 2 servings
splash of white wine
2 tsp crushed garlic
2 tsp sliced red onion
1 oz chopped green onion
8 slices red pepper
4 oz chopped spinach
pinch of Old Bay
pinch of Italian seasoning
8 oz chopped tomatoes
2 oz butter

Combine last 9 ingredients and saute for three minutes. Add scallops and simmer for two minutes. Add shrimp, feta cheese and splash of white wine and cook until shrimp are just done. Meanwhile cook fettucini until al dente, divide onto plates and spoon seafood mixture over. Serves two.

Beaufort *mm 205*

The City Docks at Beaufort, fronting blocks of art galleries, gift boutiques and antique shops is one of the most popular stops for boaters cruising the Intracoastal Waterway. Every slip is reserved for transients with expert dockmasters, fueling alongside, showers and even a courtesy car for supplies. Cafes, ice cream parlors and waterfront bars line the boardwalk where visitors may stroll and enjoy sunsets over the anchorage and late night entertainment. There are beautiful historic homes and bed and breakfast inns to tour and a maritime museum where wooden boats are handcrafted. Also within walking distance you will discover a number of excellent places to dine with a variety of cuisines from fresh seafood and regional dishes to International classics created by some masterful chefs. The following is a selection of Beaufort's better restaurants which help make this unique seaside community a must port of call for yachtsmen and visitors who love fine food.

BEAUFORT GROCERY CO.

117 Queen Street (252) 728-3899 Seasonal Closings
Lunch $6 Dinner $15 VISA MC DISC

Originally it was a grocery store serving Beaufort's historic Queen Street District just one block off the waterfront. One may still buy freshly baked breads and deli products here, but the Beaufort Grocery Co. of today is best known as one of the most popular sophisticated dining establishments in the area. Owner/chef Charles Park, a graduate of CIA and Chaine des Rotisseurs member, and his wife Wendy are always chosen as the best chefs, serving the best brunch and best seafood (not fried) and pleasing every guest every time. Like a French country bistro, you lunch on hardy home made soups and salads, deli sandwiches on oven baked breads and a variety of delectable desserts with freshly brewed coffee. Dinners are more elegant affairs with choices of premier wines to complement creative chef entrees from Chinese duck or rack of lamb to roasted pork loin or charbroiled veal chops. Daily seafood specials like pan seared salmon or grilled triggerfish with a mango coulis keep them filled nightly. They have take out baskets and will cater private parties, but Beaufort Grocery Co. is a must place to food shop.

Honey-Lemon Roasted Pork Loin

4 6 to 8 oz pork chops
1/2 cup honey
1/4 cup lemon juice
2 tblsps pine nuts
2 cups sliced kale
1/4 cup sundried tomatoes, soaked & julienned
2 tblsps olive oil
4 oz goat cheese

Saute pine nuts, kale & sundried tomatoes in oil until kale is wilted. Cool & mix with goat cheese. Debone & trim pork chops, cut slit in side and stuff with mixture. Grill pork to desired doneness, basting with honey & lemon juice glaze. Let rest 15 mins, cut on bias to show stuffing on plate & arrange over cole slaw . Serve with Harrissa & Tsatziki sauces, roasted new potatoes garnished with rosemary. Serves two.

BLUE MOON Espresso Bar & Cafe

119 Queen Street (252) 504-3036 Seasonal Closings
Bkfst $4 Lunch $ 6 Dinner $11 VISA MC

When it comes to breakfast, Blue Moon is about the only game in town and when it comes to the morning meal, this unique Espresso Bar & Cafe plays in the major league. Their kitchen starts at 5:00 am preparing dough for all their breads, muffins, scones, bagels and pastries that are served warm from the oven by opening time at 7:30. For coffee lovers, choices are unlimited from cappuccino or espresso to latte or a special plantation blend. For the hearty, you can create an omelette from a dozen different items or order eggs scrambled Turkish style with onions, garlic, tomatoes and feta. For a real southern treat, try a bowl of cheese grits with sauteed shrimp. Lunches are equally diverse with Boar's Head meats and cheeses piled high on six choices of fresh breads and rolls. Soups and salads cater to vegetarians with homemade dressings or with grilled fish or chicken. Theme nights feature sushi, Italian, Thai, Mexican or whatever Kathe and Amber Emerick and Barbara Lentz decide is fresh and fun with live music to match. You will find a cafe with cooks this creative only once in a Blue Moon!

Stuffed Pepper Soup

2 lbs ground turkey
1 tblsp olive oil
1 large white onion, diced
6 garlic cloves, minced
8 large red or green peppers, sliced
2 large can chopped tomatoes with juice
1 cup water
1/2 cup white rice
1 tsp salt
liberal dose black pepper
1 tsp tarragon
dash of cayenne pepper

Brown onion & garlic in oil, add turkey & saute until no longer pink. Add sliced peppers, tomatoes, water & uncooked rice. Add spices & let simmer approximately 1-1/2 hours. Stir frequently. Serve with fresh bread slices & garnish with strips of pepper. Serves 6 to 8.

CLAWSON'S

429 Front Street (252) 728-2133 Closed Sunday in Winter
Lunch $5 Dinner $12 VISA MC DISC

For 20 years Clawson's has been one of the most popular restaurants in Beaufort, serving homemade foods to both sailors and locals along the waterfront. Over the years it has expanded this 1905 building to include Clawson's Pub and the Fishtowne Java and Ice Cream parlor offering items to satisfy any palate or purse. Lunches from shrimp, oyster or Clawson burgers to pitas, old fashion lunch plates and stuffed potatoes called "Dirigibles" are just the beginnings of five pages of delicious choices. There are Clawson tempura veggies, cheese fries, salads, bisque and chowders, baby back ribs or steaks with bourbon, ginger or Clawson sauces. Chef Shawn Hoveland excels with specials of fresh seafood bouillons in puff pastry, sashimi tuna, crab cakes with citrus saffron sauces or mahi roulades with crab and artichoke. Wines, beers and ales, or peanut butter or mud pies with espresso cap off an evening of delightful dining in Clawson's casual, turn of the century atmosphere. Their Emporium also carries deli foods, candies and gift items to make doubly sure every guest at Clawson's leaves with tasteful memories!

Sweet Grass Jambalaya

5 oz chicken breast, cubed
3 oz smoked sausage
8 oz shrimp
1 red & yellow pepper
2 stalks celery
1 red Bermuda onion
1 lb angel hair pasta

Fry angel hair pasta in deep fryer in mesh net to make 4 baskets. Set aside to cool. For sauce, cook finely diced yellow onion in hot dry pan till almost caramelized, add 4 tblsps bacon grease, 3 tblsps thyme, 1/2 tblsp Old Bay, 1/2 tblsp cayenne & 1-1/2 cups flour. Cook till dark brown. Add 1-1/2 cups chicken stock, 2 cups white wine & cook to a thick boil. Saute chicken in olive oil with sliced sausage & chopped vegetables. Add shrimp & cook until done. Combine with sauce, pour into baskets & garnish with chopped parsley. Serves 4.

THE NET HOUSE

133 Turner Street (252) 728-2002 Closed Sunday in off season
Dinner $13 VISA MC

From outside you might mistake The Net House as just another restaurant serving lots of fried seafood, but what all locals know is nothing could be further from that image than this rustic, tinned roof building just one block from the waterfront. And once you have dined inside you too will discover why it has been the longest running and most popular restaurant in Beaufort. First of all, owners Lynda and Strug Steed, who started here in 1980 collecting loyal customers and college banners, are two of the friendliest hosts you will ever encounter. They do offer fried shrimp, flounder and shellfish, but how it's prepared and presented has few equals. Their stuffed soft shell crabs are delectable works of art as is a grouper special with a dijon topping. Most items are offered steamed, broiled or panned in butter along with soups, bisque, chowders and seafood cold plates. Lynda's mother retired from the kitchen at 91, but her homemade key lime pie is still featured. The nautical decor, like their cuisine, is kept simple and unpretentious, but The Net House is a palace for visiting sailors and any lover of fine seafood!

Net House Stuffed Soft Shell Crabs

6 softshell crabs
1 lb backfin crabmeat
1/4 cup butter
1 celery stalk
1 tblsp bell pepper
1 tblsp chopped onion
1/2 cup crushed saltines
1/2 tsp celery salt
12 tsp seafood seasoning
1 egg
1 pint milk

Finely chop onion, celery & pepper & saute in butter till soft. Mix cracker crumbs with celery salt & seafood seasoning. Combine warm milk, vegetables & crumb mixture. Add beaten egg & crabmeat & blend. Clean crabs, lift top shell & stuff with portions of mixture. Cover with shell, dip in buttermilk, flour with salt & pepper & deep fry in peanut oil, turning once. Drain & serve with lemon dill butter. Serves three.

THE VERANDA

On Taylor Creek 300 Front Street (252) 728-5352 Closed Wed.
Lunch $6 Dinner $14 VISA MC DISC

Dining at the Veranda is like visiting the Whitaker family with Tad as chef, brother Chris as host and parents Betty and Garland scurrying everywhere to assure their guests are happy. Their Veranda offers fantastic views across Taylor Creek to the ICW with magnificent sunsets for candlelight dining. Betty is responsible for the homelike decor as well as the home made biscuits, breads and salad dressings. But the spotlight has to shine on Tad, whose love for cooking is evident in every presentation from dishes of shrimp, Andouille sausage and grits to nightly specials like mixed seafood in a puff pastry with a lemon dill sauce that allows him more creativity. Although a master with seafood, his menu changes seasonally with the availability of local fish and wild game, for every item is prepared fresh to order. Homemade chutneys, salsas, unique sauces and spices embellish every steak, chicken, or pork dish, served with salads, fresh vegetables and roasted potatoes. The Whitakers want every Veranda guest to remember "how much and how good" it was to dine with them. Few, if any, could ever forget.

Sauteed Seafood in Puff Pastry

1/2 lb lrg shrimp, deveined
1/2 lb lrg sea scallops
1 lb fresh fish (tuna, mahi or grouper)
1 cup chopped scallions
1 cup mushrooms
1/4 cup butter
salt, pepper & dill to taste
1 tblsp lemon juice
1/2 cup heavy cream
4 5" puff pastry squares

Bake pastry until puffed & golden. Saute seafood, scallions & quartered mushrooms in clarified butter, add salt, pepper & dill. Add lemon juice & cream & simmer until sauce is reduced & seafood is done. Remove tops from pastry, fill with seafood mixture & replace tops. Serve with rice pilaf & sauteed vegetables. Garnish with lemon slices & fresh dill. Serves four.

Morehead City *mm 205*

At first glance Morehead City appears as just a large commercial deep water seaport where huge ships are loaded with Carolina woods, chemicals and cargo for delivery around the world. It is also the arrival and departure port for the U.S. Marine's Second Division at Camp Lejeune. But a stroll along their water front reveals an entirely new dimension to this city, with beautiful craft and gift shops, fish markets and marinas for cruising yachtsmen.

It is the homeport for fleets of charter boats with easy access to some of the best East Coast fishing grounds just offshore. They host a Big Blue Marlin tournament yearly, but you can examine fresh catches daily that are available in the local markets or as delicious entrees in some of the best restaurants on this Crystal Coast. The following have perfected the fine art of preparing seafood and offer cuisines to satisfy most any taste.

;ANITARY FISH MARKET

01 Evans Street (252) 247-3111 VISA MC DISC
unch $5 Dinner $10

he name may confuse new patrons to is restaurant until they discover that it as been called Sanitary since it began s a fish market back in 1938. Capt. Ted nd Capt. Tony added 12 bar stools that pring to become the first aterfront seafood restaurant Morehead City. Some 60 ears later the name is the ame but the Sanitary Fish larket has grown into a 500 eat restaurant that still has a aiting line in high season. The success due to Ted Garner's family continuing is tradition of preparing the freshest eafood available and serving it in large portions in spotless surroundings for a very modest price. Famous for the best fried fish, shrimp and crab cakes, their menu has also expanded to offer broiled, steamed or grilled seafood from Maine lobster to jumping mullets as well as steaks and chicken. Add daily specials and fresh veggies from okra to squash, snaps, carrots or butterbeans and their own brand of hush puppies and you understand why the walls are lined with guest photos of celebrities and beauty queens. Their Fish Market still sells fresh catches, but the Sanitary chefs are very hard to beat!

Sanitary She Crab Soup

1 lb backfin crabmeat
1/2 cup blue crab roe
4 cups whole milk
1 small can tomato soup
1 cup heavy cream
2 tblsps flour
4 tblsps butter
1 small onion
1 tblsp chives
salt & pepper to taste
dry sherry (optional)

Melt butter over low heat & add flour, stirring constantly until well blended. Add milk, heavy cream, tomato soup, chopped onion & chives & heat until mixture thickens. Do not boil. Add crabmeat, roe, salt & pepper & simmer about 30 minutes. Stir in sherry if desired just before serving. Serve with Sanitary hush puppies & garnish bowl with cilantro. Serves two.

WINDANSEA

708 Evans Street (252) 247-3000 Major Credit Cards
Dinner $15 Closed Mondays

On rare occasions you find a place like Windansea where all elements; cuisine, ambiance and service, work together to create a fantastic dining experience. The recipe is simple; rehab an old block building with brightly colored walls, paintings and pillows, build an open kitchen with a brick wood stove for all to see, add three talented chefs like Kyle, Ian and David with passions for cooking, and you have the ingredients for a restaurant filled with happy gourmands. Everything is made from scratch from lamb sausage to desserts and breads that are baked in their wood fired oven along with roasted chickens, scallops and designer pizzas. Chef Kyle transforms meats, poultry and seafood into artistic presentations that defy description, like pan seared trigger fish over cheese ravioli or grilled lamb chops with risotto and sauted okra basquaise. The wine cellar from Chilean Merlots to a Rothschild 64' is there to complement entrees, served by a bright efficient staff. Homemade desserts, cappuccino and cordials will highlight an evening of casual laid back dining guaranteed to satisfy all of your pleasure sensations.

Grilled Lamb Chops over Risotto with Okra Basquaise

8 lamb chops
1/8 cup each carrots, onion & celery, chopped
1/2 cup aborio rice
pinch saffron
4 to 6 cups chicken stock
2 cups white wine
1/2 cup fresh okra, sliced
4 tblsps roasted pepper
4 tblsps sliced shallots
pinch of thyme, sage & rosemary
4 tblsps fresh parmesan

Season chops with salt & pepper & grill to desired temp. Saute shallots in butter, add peppers, herbs & fresh okra. Saute onion, celery & onions. Add rice, chicken stock & wine slowly while stirring. Add saffron & cook rice al dente. Stir in parmesan & serve topped with chops & okra on side. Serves two.

THE PLANT

105 7th Street (252) 726-5502 VISA MC
Lunch $6 Dinner $15

The grandfather of the present owners helped Gulf Oil build this building back in 1927 as a bulk plant for fueling fishing fleets. They still pump some of the best priced fuel on the ICW but The Plant has been converted into a multi story restaurant with open decks and beautiful views of the waterway. Corinne and Paul Geer, Jr., with sons Webb and Paul, III, are still oil distributors but they now fill up hungry yachtsmen with lunches and dinners as well. They have retained the feeling of the original plant, but diesel fumes have been replaced with delicious aromas of grilled seafood, roasted prime rib and steaming bowls of shrimp. Their International menu features Polynesian, Cajun and South American dishes but changes with the seasons. They do offer fried fresh seafood as well as lunch burgers and crabcake sandwiches, but the specials like seafood pasta primavera, Cornish game hens or clams portobello make The Plant a welcome change of taste for Morehead City. On weekends their bar and warehouse fill with the sounds of live jazz, modern rock or R & B along with superb cuisine and very happy diners.

The Plant Seafood Pasta Primavera

1 doz small clams
5 oz fresh tuna
5 oz fresh mahi
4 oz fresh shrimp
2 snow crab clusters
1 cup white wine
4 oz each, carrots, red peppers, portobello mushrooms, julienned
6 oz linguine pasta
1/4 cup garlic basil pesto

Place all seafood except shrimp in pot & steam with white wine until clams open. Add shrimp & vegetables & cover & simmer 2 mins until shrimp is done. Add pesto. Cook linguine al dente & mound on plate. Arrange seafood mixture over pasta and top with snow crab legs. Top with fresh grated parmesan cheese & garnish with scallions & bean sprouts. Serves two.

CALYPSO CAFE

506 Arendell Street (252) 240-3380 VISA MC
Dinner $15 Closed Sun & Mon

After spending years in the Caribbean, it is only natural that restaurateurs David and Mary Lindsey would name their new stateside place Calypso and offer guests a real taste of the islands in their cuisine and decor. It is as casual as a barefoot, beachfront bistro with scenes of colorful West Indies homes covering the walls with tropical plants and flowers around each table. Their menu lists some typical Caribbean fare like kallaloo, an island bouillabaisse, jerk chicken with a tropical fruit salsa or angry pork with black bean sauce. They have blended these West Indian flavors with fresh produce and seafood to create tasty dishes of grilled grouper with sauteed bananas, shrimp blackened with cheddar cheese grits or shrimp curry with apples, grapes and nuts. Their specials depend on the fresh catch of the day such as grilled tuna with wasabi sauce or soft shell crabs with sundried tomatoes and portobellos over linguine. His yucca crusted triggerfish with mango relish is unbeatable with a Red Stripe beer or tropical frozen drink. Calypso is as close to the islands as your taste buds can take you...enjoy it, Mon!

Yucca Crusted Triggerfish with Black Beans & Mango Relish

4 7 oz triggerfish fillets
1 lb yucca root, peeled
1 cup flour
2 beaten eggs
4 oz butter

Dip fillets in flour, then egg then grated yucca, pressing firmly. Saute fish in butter till golden on both sides.
For relish:
Combine & chill 1 can drained black beans with 2 tblsps roasted red pepper, 1/2 chopped mango & 2 tblsps orange juice.
Arrange triggerfish on plate with bowtie pasta and sauteed yellow and green squash . Top fish with mango relish. Serves 4.

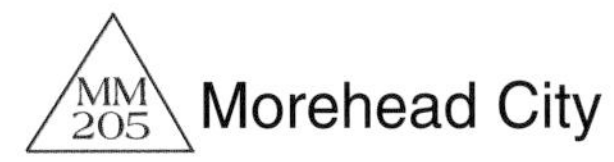

BISTRO by the SEA

4031 Arendell Street (252) 247-2777 Major Credit Cards
Dinner $12 Closed Sunday & Monday

They moved from Atlantic Beach in 1997 for more room but reservations are still recommended for parties wishing to dine at Bistro by the Sea, one of Morehead City's most uniquely elegant restaurants. It is the combined talents of owner/chef Tim Coyne and Libby Eaton and executive chef Mark Mushinski that make their Bistro so popular with locals as well as visiting gourmands lucky enough to discover them. The decor is decidedly Mediterranean but their dinner menu, featuring whatever is seasonal, defies any culinary theme. They always offer poultry, stir fries, pastas, steaks and slow roasted prime rib, but it is their specials, from a crabmeat souffle appetizer to Provimi calves liver deglazed in orange liqueur that bring out their real creativity. Salmon baked in a puff pastry with a scallop mousse, trigger fish encrusted in herbs, tuna with honey toasted almonds or seared rare with teriyaki and dill sauces are typical of daily fresh seafood features. Bistro by the Sea has a cigar patio for smokers and piano lounge for cordials or night caps after what is guaranteed to be a most memorable dining experience.

Encrusted Tuna w/ Chablis Dill Sauce

1 12 oz fresh tuna fillet, encrusted with sesame seeds & peppercorns
2 shallots, chopped fine
1 bay leaf
6 whole black peppercorns
1 clove garlic, chopped
1/2 tsp dried thyme
1 small sprig rosemary
2 fresh basil leaves
1 cup Chablis wine
3/4 cup tarragon vinegar
3 cups heavy cream
1/2 cup finely chopped dill
2 tblsps unsalted butter

Sear tuna in hot sesame oil on both sides to light brown. Combine next 9 items & reduce to almost dry. Add cream & simmer 10 mins. Strain & simmer 5 mins. Add dill, remove from heat & fold in butter. Slice tuna thin, fan on plates, add dill & teriyaki sauces. Garnish with ginger rose, roe, chives & sesame seeds. Serves 2.

Wrightsville Beach/Wilmington *mm 283*

The Cape Fear Coast, including Wrightsville, Carolina and Kure Beaches, provides 31 miles of white sand shoreline with major inlets from the Atlantic to the ICW. This Coast creates a variety of water sports from swimming, surfing and boating to fishing in protected waters or in the gulf stream offshore. With an abundance of fresh seafood and produce, the restaurants here offer guests unlimited choices of cuisine, ambiance and cost. The following are among the very best along the seashore as well as in the City of Wilmington, twelve miles up the Cape Fear River. This historic city has revitalized its downtown with galleries, shops and fine restaurants housed in restored old buildings along the waterfront. There are museums, the Battleship North Carolina and blocks of beautiful old homes on oak lined streets that make a visit here a must for any cruise along this fabulous Cape Fear Coast.

THE BRIDGE TENDER

1414 Airlie Road (910) 256-4519 Closed Sat & Sun for Lunch
Lunch $7 Dinner $18 Major Credit Cards

It is an appropriate name for a restaurant that sits right beside the ICW bridge at Wrightsville Beach, providing a perfect view of this busy waterway for dining on open decks or in air conditioned comfort inside. The Bridge Tender is renowned for seafood, but is equally famous for serving steaks and prime rib. Every meal is cooked to order and served with potatoes, rice or fresh vegetables, salad and hot baked breads. For poultry lovers, they stuff chicken breasts with crabmeat, spinach and feta cheese and top it with a lemon butter sauce for a delicious dinner entree. Chef Freddie Shaw has been delighting Bridge Tender guests for 20 years with superb dishes like Shrimp Diane, Peppered Grouper Florentine, Country Ham and Scallops or Maryland Style Crab Cakes. Managers David West and Chris Stout provide catering for special occasions at their restaurant, in their customer's homes, offices or even for private parties aboard your yacht. They have been awarded for having one of the best wine selections on the coast to complement your choice of delicious Bridge Tender culinary presentations.

Scallops & Country Ham with Pasta

1 lb medium scallops
6 oz sliced country ham
1/2 cup chopped green onions
1/2 cup sliced mushrooms
1/2 cup sundried tomatoes
4 tblsps butter
1 cup Chardonnay wine
2 tblsps cajun spice
2 cups lemon butter sauce

Cut ham slices into small bite size pieces and saute with scallops in wine & butter until scallops are just done. Add mushrooms, onions, tomatoes, spices & simmer for two minutes. Add lemon butter sauce & bring to slow boil over medium heat. Serve over bowtie or penne pasta cooked al dente. Sprinkle with grated parmesan cheese & garnish with parsley. Serves two.

PUSSER'S® at Wally's

4 Marina Street (910) 256-8500 Major Credit Cards
Lunch $7 Dinner $16

The expression, "Be there or be square" certainly applies to Pusser's at Wally's in Wrightsville Beach where every Sunday for years it is packed with boaters, bikinis, beer lovers, burgers and live bands. Now, Pusser's has added some flavors and sounds for which they are famous including a great selection of seafood and Carribean fare. Pusser's at Wally's offers three floors for dining and drinking with menus to match, from wide open decks for snacks and sandwiches to an island Pub on the second level. Fine dining on the third floor, served in an elegant island setting, offers spectacular waterfront views of sunsets and yachts on the ICW below. Their menus here combine the best of both worlds from West Indian chicken, prime rib, jerked pork chops with molasses and Pusser's Rum, to island pastas and tropical salads. They are also famous for their great seafood dishes like Caribbean glazed BBQ shrimp, Maine lobster, jerked Mahi Mahi and fresh local crab cakes. Whatever one's taste, you will find Pusser's at Wally's has the cuisine, traditions and fantastic views to satisfy.

Pusser's Carolina Crab Cakes

2 lb jumbo lump crab
2 oz bread crumbs
2 tblsps chopped parsley
3/4 cup mayonnaise
1/3 cup dijon mustard
2 oz horseradish
2 oz dry mustard
1 egg
1/2 tblsp black pepper
1/2 tblsp celery salt
1 tsp garlic powder

Combine all ingredients except crab meat & bread crumbs to make a wet mix. Gently fold mixture into crab meat taking care not to break up lumps. Carefully fold bread crumbs into crab mixture. Cover bowl & refrigerate for 1/2 hour. Scoop out 4 oz portions & flatten into patties. Pan fry in virgin olive oil until golden brown on both sides. Serve with Tropical cole slaw. Serves four.

KING NEPTUNE

11 North Lumina Avenue (910) 256-2525 AE VISA MC
Dinner $12

The huge smiling sunshine face over the entrance and the brightly colored exterior are clues to the ambiance and cuisine awaiting every patron at this festive King Neptune restaurant. Owners Pam and Bernard Carroll take their staff to the islands and return with new authentic Caribbean recipes and laid back island attitudes. This fun loving family of chefs, cooks, hosts and waitresses makes dining here as delicious and casual as sitting on a tropical beach. Jerked chicken or tuna, curried or coconut shrimp, Rasta Pasta or Voodoo snapper are typical of the West Indian flavors offered on their fun to read menus. Their house specialties feature Creole shrimp over grits, grilled lemon chicken, blackened grouper or one may order prime rib or a giant chopped steak. The adjacent lounge is like a pirate ship with flags, swords and lanterns on the walls and a variety of rums at the bar. The Carroll's are enjoying a childhood dream of treating their guests to a rare taste of Caribbean life with delicious dishes and fun. Fourth graders designed their kids menu to make King Neptune a great island visit for the entire family. It is that!

King Neptune's Curried Island Shrimp

1 lb 20/25 count shrimp
4 oz clarified butter
1/2 each yellow onion, red, green & yellow peppers
1 Habanaro pepper
1/2 zucchini
1 stalk broccoli
2 tblsps curry powder

Slice onion, peppers & squash, cut broccoli into florets, seed & slice Habanaro pepper & saute all in butter until just tender. Peel & devein shrimp, leaving tails on & add to vegetables with 1/4 cup water & simmer till done. Add curry powder & simmer till thickened. Serve shrimp & vegetable mixture over 4 cups cooked sunshine rice seasoned with 1 tblsp onion powder, pinch of turmeric, salt & pepper to taste. Serves four.

CAROLINA'S

1610 Pavilion Place (910) 256-5008 VISA MC AE
Lunch $6 Dinner $16

It is hard to imagine a restaurant serving dishes as sophisticated as one finds at Carolina's, initially started as a sandwich and sub shop not too many years ago. Ann Tobin and Joe Gondek still offer this lighter fare for lunches with open face pitas, burgers and superb soups, homemade by Ann's mother. This menu is also served in their adjacent sportsbar called "Sidelines" that has TV football nights, pool tables and live bands on weekends. But for truly remarkable gourmet dining, you must try Carolina's in the evening with candlelight, sculptured artworks and superb service. It is here one discovers the talents and recipes of Ann, who will marinate a free range chicken for days, stuff spinach and cheese under the skin and then roast it to perfection. Their Scallops Josef with a ginger cream sauce, Lamb Wellington, pan seared filet mignon with a gorgonzola cheese crust or the Grouper Francais are only examples of nightly specials. Joe's wine cellar is exceptional and he lets guests bring in new vintages, if he gets a taste! Ann says Carolina's is "where you pay for food, not the view". She is so right!

Rosemary & Garlic Marinated Lamb Chops

1 rack lamb, French cut
olive oil
rosemary
2 potatoes
1/2 vidalia onion
2 roma tomatoes
1 cup yellow corn
garlic whipped potatoes

Marinate lamb chops in olive oil, rosemary & garlic for 24 hours. Pan sear chops in smoking hot pan in olive oil. Add quartered potatoes & vedalia onion & roast at 500 degrees for 6 minutes. Remove lamb to rest, add corn to pan & heat through. Arrange chops over garlic mashed potatoes & add roasted potatoes, onion & corn. Sauce is Marsala infused lamb stock & butter. Serves two.

DOCKSIDE

Dockside Marina 1308 Airlie Road *(910) 256-2752 VISA MC DISC*
Lunch $5 Dinner $12

What used to be a wild bar stop on the ICW that sold fuel, bait and tackle has evolved over the years to become a popular family restaurant, where the kids can get a hot dog while parents dine on great seafood platters. They still pump fuel and still have two bars inside that jump with local sailors, film makers and live music on the weekends. Rebuilt after Hurricane Fran it now offers large open decks and glass enclosed dining upstairs for boat and people watching overlooking the waterway. The menu has expanded as well to include broiled or grilled fresh catches of the day as well as steamed clams, shrimp or crab legs. Dockside has also instituted special Southwestern evenings, oyster festivals and steamed crab nights in addition to chicken, pastas and salads and the best Carolina hamburger you will find anywhere. Boaters may tie up free for dining and a few transient slips handle cruisers wanting to sample Cape Fear cuisine and some southern hospitality. Dockside delivers all of the above with good food and a super friendly staff that makes dining and partying here a time to remember!

Grilled Mahi-Mahi with Ginger Sauce

2 lbs Mahi fillets
(grouper or lite flavor fish may be substituted)
1 medium ginger root
10 oz teriyaki sauce
1/2 cup olive oil
1/2 bunch green onions

Peel ginger root and grate finely. Finely chop onions including tops. Combine ginger & onions with olive oil and teriyaki sauce and mix well or puree in blender. Heat mixture to boiling, strain and chill. Brush sauce on fillets, continue to baste while grilling on both sides until just done. Serve mahi fillets with rice pilaf and fresh steamed broccoli, carrots and squash. Place sauce on side for dipping fillets and garnish with lemon wedges.
Serves four.

WATER STREET

5 South Water Street (910) 343-0042 Major Credit Cards
Lunch $6 Dinner $12

At the door you come face to face with a Bengal tiger saying, "Pat Me For Good Luck". If you are fortunate enough to have found this restaurant and sidewalk cafe, then your "good luck" has already begun, for this is perhaps the funkiest and most entertaining place on the waterfront. It is an old warehouse filled with maritime memorabilia that is reminiscent of Wilmington's busy river port days. It is also a center stage for the performing arts with live jazz, flamenco guitarists and Dixieland bands featured weekly. As for the food, it is as diverse and exciting as the surroundings with lunch choices of black bean burritos or gyros and other unique specials. For dinner, Chef Julian Harris creates delicious entrees including chargrilled beef tournedos served with a wild mushroom and sundried tomato sauce, or sauteed chicken breast with broccoli florets in a parmesan cream sauce. For vegetarians the grilled portobello or eggplant sandwiches with goat cheese are exceptional as well as their cream of artichoke soup. Owner Harper Peterson has created a setting at Water Street that recaptures those bawdy riverfront days!

Red Snapper Over Rosemary Potatoes

2 7 oz red snapper fillets
2 large garlic cloves
1/4 cup white wine
juice of 1 lemon
2 tomatoe slices
flour
olive oil
salt & pepper to taste

Smother snapper fillets with crushed garlic, salt & peppr to taste. Lightly flour & pan sear in smoking pan with olive oil on one side. Flip & deglaze with lemon juice & white wine. Place tomato slice on top & bake 2 mins at 425 degrees. Meanwhile boil 5 red skin potatoes till done. Mash with 4 tblsps roasted garlic, 5 tblsps butter, 1/4 cup milk & fresh rosemary, salt & pepper to taste. Mound potatoes on plates & top with shredded parmesan. Place fillet over & serve with sauteed green peas. Serves two.

CAFFÈ PHOENIX

9 South Front Street (910) 343-1395 Major Credit Cards
Lunch $6 Dinner $14 Closed Sunday Lunch

Over eight years ago, Michael and Deborah Caliva started a news stand in an 1899 warehouse and opened a small neighborhood cafe. With little restaurant experience but with a love of good food and wine they created one of the most uniquely successful dining establishments in this city. There is this visually appealing freshness in the decor, ambiance and cuisine at Caffe Phoenix that makes it a favorite of locals, movie stars and any visiting gourmet lucky enough to find them. How would you describe a cafe that serves English herb teas as well as Dr. Brown sodas, that will pour a 1994 French Merlot by the glass or prepare special menus featuring Greek, Asian, Indian or French cuisine on weekends. Lunches and dinners have an Italian flair but are equally diverse with local produce and seafood served with salads, pastas and hot baked breads. Their horseradish, dijon encrusted salmon with a dill sauce over linguine is a delicious sample from their talented chef, Nancy. Like the mythical bird Phoenix, this reborn, one of a kind Caffe has breathed new life into the culinary taste of historic Wilmington!

Horseradish/Dijon Encrusted Salmon w/ Dill Beurre Blanc

4 7 oz salmon fillets
1 cup prepared horseradish
1 cup country style dijon
1/2 cup fresh bread crumbs
1 tblsp thyme
4 tblsps butter
1 egg

Brush salmon with beaten egg & coat top with mix of horseradish, dijon, bread crumbs & thyme. Sear fillets in butter, coated side first till brown, turn for 10 seconds. For dill sauce: combine 3 sliced shallots, 1/2 cup white wine, 2 tblsps dill & cook till almost evaporated. Add 1 cup heavy cream & reduce until thickened. Lower to simmer & whisk in butter. Finish fish in 400 degree oven & serve over garlic mashed potatoes & asparagus. Drizzle sauce on top. Serves four.

THE PHARMACY

110 East Moore Street (910) 457-5577 VISA MC DISC
Lunch $6 Dinner $16 Closed Sunday

In 1887, a local doctor began dispensing pills to his patients in this building which has been known as the Pharmacy ever since. Today however, patrons at The Pharmacy restaurant are only served potions guaranteed to satisfy any appetite or any palate. No physician, but chef Philip Phipps' prescriptions will cure anyone's craving for lunch or dinner with his homemade soups and fresh garden salads, incredible entrees and desserts to die for. Well tutored by his father and brother at Mr. P's Bistro, Philip's inherited love of cooking shows in his presentations of low country crabcakes, shrimp and scallops meuniere or his roast pork loin with a brandy dijon sauce. His seafood okra gumbo, blue crab soup and tomato Florentine are superb, but locals request notification when his shrimp bisque is on the menu. His pan seared salmon over braised spinach with a tomato caper beurre blanc or his shrimp over pasta with a Chardonnay sauce are perfect remedies for seafood lovers. The Phipps family at Mr. P's Bistro and The Pharmacy are a culinary credit to the city of Southport. One must dine at both!

Sauteed Shrimp w/ Chardonnay Sauce

3 dozen large shrimp
1/4 cup white wine
8 artichoke hearts
1/2 leek
4 cups Chardonnay
2 cups fish stock
1/2 quart heavy cream
capellini for four

For sauce:
Reduce Chardonnay to a glaze. Add fish stock & reduce again to a glaze. Add cream & reduce until thickened.
Peel & devein shrimp & saute in 1 tsp olive oil until pink. Splash with wine & add sliced artichoke hearts & leeks, blanched & sliced. Reduce mix & salt & pepper to taste. Spoon over capellini & top with grated Asiago cheese. Serve with sauteed squash, red peppers, broccoli & carrots. Serves four.

MR. P'S BISTRO

309 North Howe Street (910) 457-0832 Major Credit Cards
Dinner $18 Closed Sunday

When you hear a professional chef say, "Nothing makes me happier than to just cook", you can be certain any dish they present will be exceptional. Stephen L. Phipps, who began in his teens, attended culinary school and then trained under master chefs for years, has a passion for cooking that makes Mr. P's Bistro a rare find in small cities like Southport. But Stephen returned to his roots, joined his father's restaurant and has been changing the culinary habits of his patrons with creative dishes ever since. Marinated duck, shad roe with country ham, crab stuffed quail or flounder with sesame shrimp are examples that would satisfy any gourmet. Stephen adds his personal touch to recipes he learned in Charleston. He grills beef tenderloins topped with sea scallops, crabmeat and a roasted pepper hollandaise, or he will debone and pan sear a marinated rack of lamb that would bring rave reviews even in New York's finest. Mr. P's portions are large, including an Oyster Bienville appetizer that is a meal in itself. Southport can be proud of Mr. P's fine dining and their Phipps family of chefs!

Mr. P's Oysters Bienville

4 doz oysters on halfshell
1 lb shrimp, cooked
1 cup each, flour, butter & heavy cream
2 cups chopped shallots
1/2 cup chopped parsley
3 tsps chopped garlic
3 cups milk
8 egg yolks
1/2 cup dry sherry
2 tsps each salt & pepper
1 tsp cayenne pepper
1-1/2 cups mushrooms
fresh grated Asiago cheese

Saute shallots, parsley & garlic in butter till soft. Add flour & cook 5 mins to make a roux. Add milk & cream & cook till smooth. Mix egg yolks, sherry & seasoning together & add to mixture while stirring. Add chopped mushrooms & shrimp, cook till thickened, pour out & let set. Top oysters with mix & Asiago & bake at 450 till brown. Serves eight.

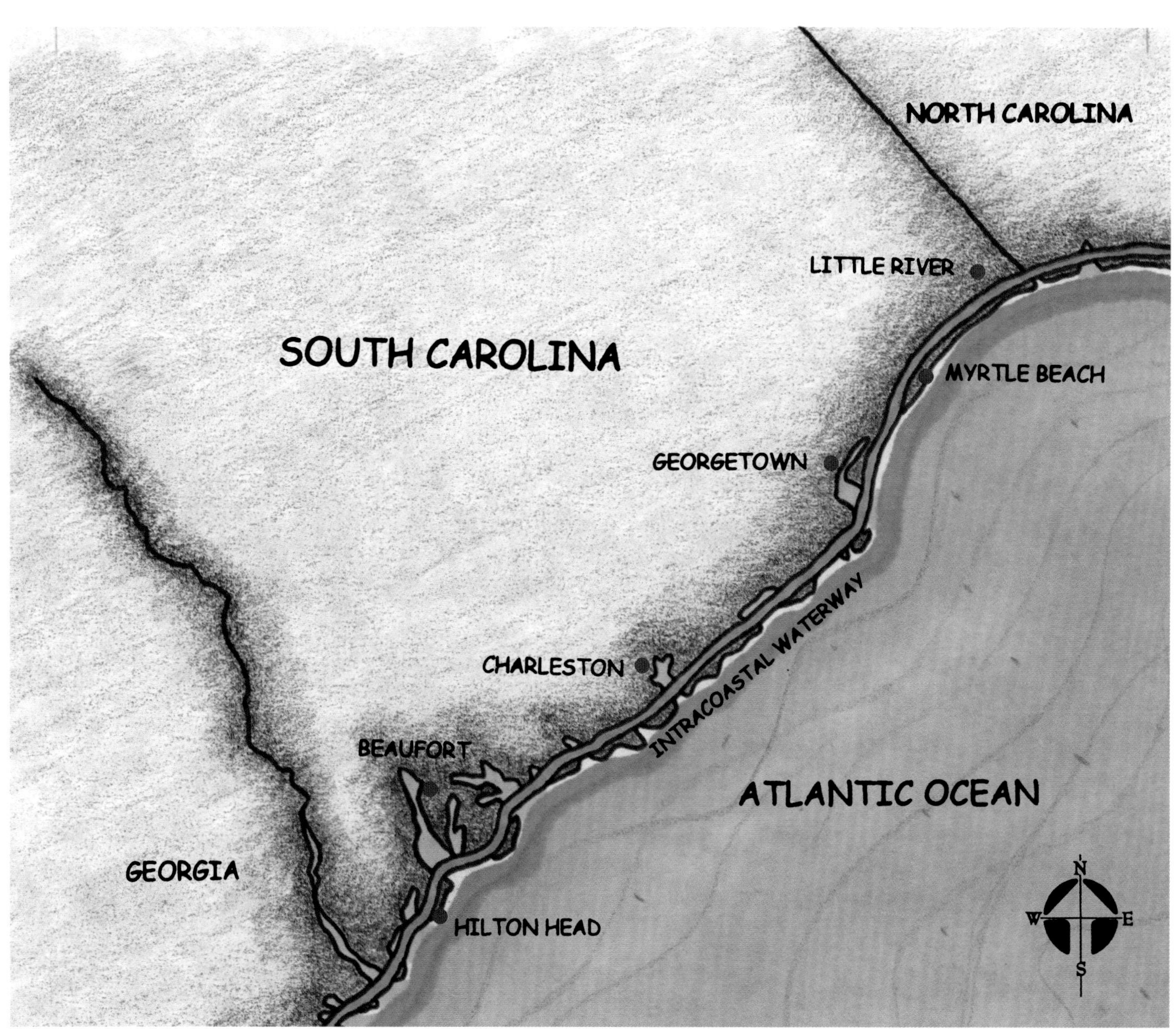
NORTH CAROLINA
LITTLE RIVER
SOUTH CAROLINA
MYRTLE BEACH
GEORGETOWN
INTRACOASTAL WATERWAY
CHARLESTON
BEAUFORT
ATLANTIC OCEAN
GEORGIA
HILTON HEAD
N
W
E
S

SOUTH CAROLINA *mm 342 to 576*

You have to wonder as you travel through South Carolina if this state has more people playing golf or more catching shrimp. Here the Intracoastal Waterway is lined on both sides with hundreds of beautiful courses and waters are filled with boats casting nets for those delicious crustaceans. Besides golfing, fishing and beachcombing, the Grand Strand area of Myrtle Beach has become a meca for outlet shopping and entertainment with Broadway shows and country western st[illegible] Dolly Parton to Kenny Rogers. F[illegible] finds quieter waterfront towns like G[illegible] and Beaufort and magnificient Charles[illegible] that is the epitome of gracious southern livi[illegible] The lifestyles, activities and terrain found along this South Carolina Coast are as varied as the cuisines travelers will enjoy from low country cooking to highly sophisticated gourmet dining.

DOWN UNDER

Hwy 17 & McCorsley Ave. (843) 249-5110 Major Credit Cards
Lunch $6 Dinner $16 Closed Sunday & Monday

If he is not cooking, owner Allan Pratt will greet you with a typical Australian "G' Day Mate" welcome to his Deli and Restaurant that is filled with Down Under memorabilia and lots of really good stuff to eat. There are maps, flags boomerangs, sailing photos of the Aussie's America's Cup winner and even a live baby crocodile that seems to say, "Let's party, mate and have some non-serious fun"! In fact the only thing they are serious about at Down Under is their cuisine and making sure every patron leaves full and happy. Lunches feature homemade soups and deli sandwiches from two-handed Aussie clubs to Reubens along with chicken, shrimp or chef salads made fresh daily. Full course gourmet dinners are a blend of French, Australian and Island recipes Allan creates from freshly cut meats, fowl and seafood. Try his Steak Diane, or Pork with a Marsala apple glaze, or his Scallops with Jamaican relish or the Chicken with a Mango chutney sauce and then you'll know why this small but intimate little bit of Down Under is so popular with serious diners. Allan will fetch fellow sailors from nearby marinas...call for a "G' Day Mate".

Down Under Grouper with Mango Chutney

4 8 oz grouper fillets
garlic salt
black pepper
flour
2 lbs fresh mangoes
1 tsp crushed garlic
1/2 tsp crushed ginger
2 tblsps olive oil
1 tblsp vinegar
1 tsp crushed dried chilies

Lightly dredge grouper fillets in flour seasoned with garlic salt & pepper. Saute in oil & butter until golden crisp on both sides. For sauce, peel mangoes & slice into julienne strips. Add garlic, ginger, olive oil, vinegar & chillies & blend well. Store chilled. Arrange sauteed fillets on plates & spoon mango chutney over. (Chutney also goes well with battered shrimp or chicken strips). Serves 4.

UMBERTO'S

Coquina Harbor 720 Highway 17 North (843) 249-5552 AE VISA MC
Dinner $17 Closed Sundays in Winter

There is a saying that after eating at this restaurant you tend to get hungry again in four or five days! Not only is the Italian cuisine superb, but the portions are so large you can enjoy it on your yacht or at home again and again. Over the years Umberto's has become so popular with transient boaters and golfers, that they plan their trips just to dine here. Owner Jacqui Isbill, a former model, nurse and artist, treats her patrons as family and friends and serves them four course dinners in beautiful surroundings with views of Coquina Harbor. Jacqui's kitchen hand-cuts all their meats and fish, providing triple size lamb, pork and veal chops from 32 to 38 ounces and oversized salmon fillets. Her menu features all the classics from Chicken Marsala and Veal Piccata to Steak Scampi and Grouper Umberta with white wine, artichokes, black olives and jumbo shrimp. Her Italian Family Feast consists of three appetizers, capelleni, Minestra beans, Ceasar salad, chicken Cacciatori, pork chops and Ossobuco for a modest price. This is a self portrait of Jacqui, a talented restaurateur and delightful host.

Grouper Umberta

2 8 oz grouper fillets
8 jumbo shrimp
4 artichoke hearts
2 tblsps sliced black olives
salt & pepper to taste
1 tblsp Italian seasoning
juice of 1/2 lemon
1/4 cup white wine
clarified butter
flour

Dredge fish fillets in flour and saute in clarified butter. Turn once and sprinkle with seasonings. When half done add shrimp, shelled and cleaned and saute with quartered artichoke hearts and black olives. When fillets are lightly colored add dash of lemon juice and deglaze with white wine. Place fillets on plate and spoon shrimp sauce over. Serve with roasted red potatoes and garnish with parsley. Serves two.

SANTE FE STATION

Highway 17 & 11th Avenue North (843) 249-3463 AE VISA MC
Dinner $13

For over 20 years people have been making tracks to this restaurant to enjoy some of the best southwestern cuisine this side of Sante Fe. While noted for their steaks, prime rib and baby back ribs they are equally adept in preparing fresh seafood with a few cajun touches. Sante Fe Station opens for passengers at four daily with early bird specials and happy hours for half price drinks, salsa dips, spicy buffalo wings and chilled raw bar appetizers. Like the old dining cars, their menu offers everything from snacks and salads to gourmet locomotive burgers, Mexican potato skins or a chicken and rib platter smoked in-house. For lovers of seafood there's shrimp, lobster, crab dishes and Oysters Sante Fe that are superb. You can add a steak or chicken to most any seafood entree to satisfy both cravings. Chef Buddy Cribb, whose railroad buff father started Sante Fe, and partner D.J. Karavan serve patrons large portions of well prepared food in a fun filled train station atmosphere. If you have a taste for a culinary side trip and some great Southwestern style cuisine, "Climb Aboard" at this Sante Fe Station.

Baked Oysters Sante Fe

16 select oysters
1/2 lb lump crab meat
1 onion, chopped fine
1/2 cup finely chopped red & green peppers
2 tblsps mustard
2 tblsps mayonnaise
1 tblsp Old Bay
1/4 cup parsley flakes
1 egg, beaten

Open shells leaving oysters in bottom half. Combine remaining ingredients & top oysters with mixture. Place oysters under broiler until brown. Blend together 1 cup heavy cream, 2 tblsps butter, 3 tblsps grated parmesan & 2 tblsps pesto paste. Top oysters with pesto sauce & grated jack cheese & broil again until crunchy brown. Garnish with lemon slices & parsley flakes. Serves two.

THE PINK MAGNOLIA

719 Front Street (843) 527-6506 Major Credit Cards
Lunch $6 Dinner $10

The river seems to end at a huge steel mill, making first time visitors to historic Georgetown wonder about the quality of life to be found here. But just one visit to The Pink Magnolia will prove that this waterfront town is as healthy, charming and culinary sophisticated as any stop along the ICW. It can all be attributed to Myra and Bill Johnson, native Georgetonians who began catering some ten years ago so successfully they opened Pink Magnolia by local demand. "Fine Southern Cuisine" is an understatement for Myra's homestyle chicken pot pie or fried chicken salad served with special potato wedges over mixed greens. Her Carolina seafood gumbo or black bean cakes, blooming onions or the sherried crab in a puff pastry are astounding as well as fresh desserts of bread pudding, kiwi strawberry cake and bourbon pecan pie to equal your Mom's best! Bill, as the perfect host, makes everyone feel welcome in their town and Pink Magnolia, while Myra's cooking assures their return. They will cater parties for your boat or on shore, but for the best dining around, sail into Georgetown and meet Myra and Bill!

Kiwi & Strawberry Layer Cake

3 kiwi fruit, peeled
12 fresh strawberries
1 pt ricotta cheese
1 cup confectionery sugar
1/2 tsp cinnamon
3 1" yellow cake layers
3 cups white cake frosting

Blend ricotta cheese, sugar & cinnamon together & spread half on cake layer. Top with sliced fresh strawberries. Add second cake layer & spread with remaining filling. Top with peeled & sliced kiwi fruit. Add third cake layer. Cover cake with 1 cup white cake frosting. Blend pink food coloring to 1 cup frosting & spoon on top. Blend green food coloring to remaining cup of frosting & add to topping. Slice cake & serve with slices of fresh strawberries & kiwi fruit. Serves 8 to 10.

Charleston *mm 469*

Charleston is without question the Grand Dame of all southern cities, for it has maintained that special charm and gentility, along with beautiful colonial and antebellum architecture through hurricanes and wars for centuries. Originally settled in 1670, Charleston today is a "living museum" offering visitors historic scenes from the Revolution and Civil wars to fighting ships of WW II. There are plantations and garden tours for fascinating glimpses of the past with all the modern amenities for recreation and relaxation one could desire. The area's sunny beaches, world class golfing, charter fishing and shopping in open air markets, art galleries and craft shops make Charleston the perfect vacation destination. For dining, few places compare with the diversity of cuisine offered, from low country cooking to fine continental dining in elegant settings. The restaurants of Charleston are among this Nation's very best.

THE BOATHOUSE at Breach Inlet

101 Palm Blvd. Isle of Palms (843) 866-8000 AE VISA MC
Dinner $11

Perched high on pilings, The Boathouse provides wide panoramic views from the Atlantic to the Intracoastal Waterway less than 100 yards away. It is where guests watch the Charleston skyline aglow at sunset while dining on some of the freshest seafood found anywhere, prepared to be as tasteful and pleasing as the surrounding scenery. As a relatively new restaurant they have simplified their menu to offer steaks and chicken while featuring daily caught fish, lobster, scallops and shrimp. They are extremely proud of their shrimp and stone ground grits with Andouille sausage and claim to have the best crab cakes south of Maryland. Mahi-Mahi, yellowfin tuna, grouper and Atlantic salmon, purchased daily and never frozen, are grilled or blackened and served with a choice of homemade sauces. Their shellfish combination, piled high with mussels, scallops, clams, lobster tail, sausage and peppers in marinara over linguine is a bargain-priced delicious specialty. The Boathouse offers inboard and outboard dining, dockage for small boats, courtesy rides from local marinas and fresh seafood at its best!!

Boathouse Shrimp, Sausage & Grits

14 medium shrimp
1/4 lb Andouille sausage
1 cup mixed peppers & onions, sliced thin
3 tblsps olive oil
2 garlic cloves, minced
Cajun & Old Bay seasoning
2 cups cooked grits
2 Roma tomatoes
colored peppercorns
salt
green Tabasco sauce

Heat olive oil in sautee pan. Add peppers, onions, garlic & chopped sausage & cook until almost done. Shell & clean shrimp & add to pan with Cajun, Old Bay, salt & pepper. Cook until pink but not overdone. Spread grits on plates & spoon shrimp mixture over. Sprinkle with chopped tomatoes & fresh herbs & garnish with green Tabasco sauce.
Serves two.

SLIGHTLY UP THE CREEK

130 Mill Street Mt. Pleasant (843) 884-5005 Major Credit Cards
Dinner $11

The expression, "Up the creek without a paddle", usually means you're lost and have missed the proverbial boat, but in this case it simply means you've found the finest dining restaurant on Shem Creek in the historic fishing village of Mt. Pleasant. Two dining levels provide guests with views of the Charleston Harbor and shrimp boats lining the creek, and in warm months you can enjoy frozen drinks, lite menu items and sunsets from their waterfront bar, "Without a Paddle". The menu designed by Chef Frank Lee, who also directs the kitchen at Slightly North of Broad, offers Southern regional dishes that feature fresh seafood. Cajun spiced dolphin over local greens, grilled quail over grits with black eyed peas, or their spicy Pad Thai rice noodle dish with shrimp and pork are typical of his Maverick style cooking. We should also mention they serve one of the best Martinis in town...but if you're either sailor or landlubber looking for really delicious food and wine at most reasonable prices in a picturesque waterfront setting, then we recommend you drive or sail Slightly Up The Creek, with or without a paddle!

Poached Mussels with White Wine, Garlic & Parsley

20 cleaned mussels
2 tsps butter
1/2 tsp chopped garlic
1/2 cup chopped parsley
1 cup dry, white wine
salt & pepper to taste

Melt butter in large skillet and add garlic, parsley, wine and a pinch of salt and pepper and mussels. Cover and cook over high heat for three minutes, occasionally shaking the pan, until mussels open. To serve, arrange mussels in a soup plate or pasta bowl and pour sauce over. Garnish dish with fresh chopped tomato, grated Parmesan cheese and chopped parsley. Serve with crusty sourdough bread and a glass of fume blanc. Serves two as an appetizer.

ROCKFISH GRILLE

Charleston Harbor Hilton Resort, 20 Patriots Point Rd (843) 856-0028
Bkfst$8 Lunch $8 Dinner $15

The Rockfish Grille is part of a beautiful Hilton Resort overlooking the Charleston Harbor at Patriots Point. It is the culinary center for this luxury hotel complex that includes a private sand beach with palm trees, pool, an adjoining golf course and the largest and most modern marina in the Carolinas. With over 450 slips it is the ideal port of call, convenient to the open ocean or Intracoastal Waterway and Charleston, minutes away by water taxi. In a Caribbean style atmosphere, Chef Chris Orcutt caters to boaters, golfers or hungry travelers with delicious choices from a Plantation Breakfast or a Fried Oyster Po Boy for lunch, to an Orange Infused Muscovy Duck Breast for dinner. His fresh seafood entrees, Crabcakes, panseared Tuna, coriander crusted Mahi or linguine Cioppino are all exceptional as is their BBQ stuffed veal chop or beef filet with a Creole bordelaise. A light menu and outside dining are available at their Hog Island Bar with sportsfishing decor. This resort at Patriots Point with the Links, Hilton Hotel and Charleston Harbor Marina adds a new dimension to this area for sports lovers and gourmets.

Sauteed Crabcakes w/ Habanero Tartar

1 lb lump crabmeat
1 cup mayonnaise
1 egg white
1/4 cup fine cracker meal
1/2 tblsp dry mustard
1/2 tblsp cayenne pepper
1/2 tblsp Old Bay seasoning
juice of 2 lemons
2 cups bread crumbs
1 cup olive oil

Whip mayonnaise, egg white, lemon juice & dry seasoning together. Fold in crabmeat & cracker meal. Make 4 oz crab cakes, roll in breadcrumbs & saute on both sides in hot olive oil till crispy brown. Serve over tartar sauce with habanero pepper added & top with fresh tomato salsa. Serve with garlic mashed potatoes & sauteed spinach. Serves four.

CHARLESTON GRILL

Charleston Place 130 Market Street (843) 577-4522 Major Credit Cards
Dinner $19

For five years in a row Charleston Place has been voted one of the finest hotels in the world and ranks in the best top 10 for North America. It is little wonder that their Charleston Grill would be equally honored in a City noted for excellence in fine restaurants and cuisine. The Grill itself is a delight to enter with warm mahogany walls, a palm lined courtyard and Vintner's Room filled with select wines. The soft sounds of jazz complement an evening of exceptional dining. It is the perfect setting for the presentations of Chef Bob Waggoner whose years in France taught him how to combine the finest ingredients in unique new ways. Appetizers of escargot over truffle grits or young zucchini blossoms stuffed with lobster, entrees of lamb tenderloin over braised eggplant, duck confit over caramelized Vidalias and Carolina rabbit loin in puff pastry are delicious examples of his creativity. The Grill is notable for after dinner wines, cordials, fine cigars and for Plantation Suppers on Sunday featuring Lowcountry cuisine with a French flair. It is Charleston's leading dining destination!

Escargots and Chanterelles over Truffled Grits

12 escargot
8 small chanterelles
6 tblsps grits
2 cups milk
2 tblsps fresh truffels
4 tsp butter
1 garlic clove, chopped fine
1 cup chicken stock

Cook grits in milk with 2 tsps butter until done. Add finely chopped truffels and keep warm. Pan sear escargots in 2 tsp butter & brown lightly on each side. Add chanterelles & finely chopped garlic clove. Remove & deglaze pan with chicken stock & reduce to sauce consistency. Divide grits into serving cups & arrange escargot & mushroom on top. Spoon sauce over & garnish with thin chive tips. Serves two.

PENINSULA GRILL

Planters Inn 112 North Market Street (843) 723-0700
Dinner $20 Major Credit Cards

In less than a year the Peninsula Grill has received rave reviews from Atlanta to Los Angeles and was listed as one of Esquire's Best New Restaurants of 1997. It has been called Charleston's hottest new dining spot, clubby and sophisticated without being stuffy. It is all that and more, for where does one find fried green tomatoes served with Beluga caviar and quail eggs, martinis poured from silver shakers, Dom Perignon by the glass and a wait staff so attentive you would swear they were all Paris trained. Velvet walls hung with oil paintings provide muted colors and soft sounds that compliment the inventive cuisines of chef Robert Carter, one of the country's leading culinary talents. From his Wild Mushroom Grits and Lowcountry Oyster Stew to Benne Crusted Rack of Lamb, his menu is a reflection of classic supper club dining of the 1940's. An award winning wine cellar and bar that creates perfect Manhattans are the work of GM Andrew Fallen, whose attention to detail makes all the elements come together to create an evening of truly memorable dining. In the historic Planters Inn, Peninsula Grill is simply one of Charleston's very best!

Low Country Oyster Stew w/ Wild Mushroom Grits

16 oysters with liquor
1 slice bacon, diced
1 tblsp diced Vidalia onion
1 tblsp minced garlic
2 tblsps sweet corn
2 tblsps minced red, yellow & green bell peppers
1/2 cup chicken stock
1/4 cup heavy cream
2 tblsps basil, chopped
2/3 cups grits cooked with wild mushrooms

Fry bacon till crisp & add onion & garlic & saute until clear. Add corn, peppers & saute 1 minute. Add stock, heavy cream, basil & reduce until thick. Season with salt & pepper, add oysters & simmer until edges curl. Scoop 2 tblsps grits in middle of 4 bowls, spoon stew around & place 4 oysters in each bowl. Serves four.

ELLIOTT'S On The Square

387 King Street at the Francis Marion Hotel (843) 724-8888
Brkfst $5 Lunch $7 Dinner $18 Major Credit Cards

Following the successes of its two other restaurants, the Elliott Group opened a third at the historic Francis Marion Hotel on King Street and named it Elliott's on the Square. Where the decor and cuisine at their Slightly North of Broad and Slightly Up The Creek have held to Charleston tradition, this newest venture has become another Maverick with its Art Deco designs, original paintings, unique fabrics and a menu that is more contemporary than southern. From a breakfast of French toast or Belgian waffles, a shrimp tart or smoked chicken plate for lunch to dinner entrees of herb crusted sea bass or roast veal chops, the menus are outstanding in every way.

The unpretentious cooking style of chef Frank McMahon, a CIA graduate, transforms fresh ingredients and products into flavors approaching "culinary heaven". His tuna tartare, lamb loin and duck confit with goat cheese fritter provide a unique change of taste to Charleston's traditional cuisine. The perfection of Elliott's on the Square in cuisine, service and ambiance is a fitting tribute to owner Richard D. Elliott, Maverick restaurateur!

Tuna Tartare

8 oz bigeye tuna
1/2 oz diced black olives
1 oz tomato, diced fine
1 tblsp each finely diced coriander, chives, chervil
2 tblsps virgin olive oil
kosher salt
cracked black pepper
grated lemon zest
8 French bread croutons

Dice tuna into 1/4" pieces & mix with olives, tomatoes & herbs. Toss with olive oil, salt, pepper & lemon zest. Set aside.
For vinaigrette: Whisk together 2 tblsps balsamic vinegar, 2 tblsps sherry wine vinegar, salt & pepper to taste. Slowly whisk in 1 cup extra virgin olive oil. Mound tuna mixture on croutons & drizzle lightly with vinaigrette. Garnish with fresh herbs & toast points. Serves four.

SLIGHTLY NORTH OF BROAD

192 East Bay Street (843) 723-3424 Major Credit Cards
Lunch $7 Dinner $13 Closed for Lunch Sat. & Sun.

The name actually refers to its location in downtown Charleston, but to locals it is affectionately called S.N.O.B. However, everything about this "Maverick Southern Kitchen", its decor, ambiance and especially the cuisine, defies that description. Residing in a 19th century warehouse with high ceilings and exposed heart pine beams, it creates a sense of southern hospitality that is friendly and warm but far from staid. For this is "One happening place!", with an open kitchen under a brick arch where scents, sights and sounds are shared between guests and staff. The maestro of this culinary concert is Frank Lee, a French trained chef with a "maverick" style of Southern cooking. He will top BBQ tuna with fried oysters, country ham and green onions, stuff quail with spicy sausage and serve it over butterbeans, or place crab cakes on grilled tenderloins with bearnaise. From his Charleston okra soup or Maverick paté to a classic Thai dish or Lowcountry sampler, you can count on combinations and flavors unique and exceptional. For slightly sophisticated dining, Slightly North of Broad is one unexpected sensation!

Grilled BBQ Tuna

4 5 oz tuna loins
2 cups cornmeal
2 dozen oysters
4 oz country ham, Julienne
8 oz chicken stock
1/2 cup green onions
4 oz unsalted butter
2 cups mustard Q sauce

Cook ham in stock & reduce by 1/2. Whisk in butter & add chopped onions. Brush tuna with olive oil & grill till medium rare. For Q sauce mix 1-1/4 cups each vinegar & mustard, 1/4 cup ketchup, 1/2 cup each honey & water & 1 tblsp each Tabasco & Worcestershire. Bring to a boil & cool. Coat tuna with Q sauce & glaze over med heat. Roll oysters in corn meal & pan fry in hot oil for 40 secs. Place tuna over Q sauce & top with oysters, ham & onion butter. Garnish with chopped green onions. Serves four.

BLOSSOM CAFE

171 East Bay Street (843) 722-9200 Major Credit Cards
Lunch $8 Dinner $14

Whereas Magnolias is the epitome of Southern charm and elegance, Blossom Cafe is the dazzling sister with Art Deco decor, an exhibition kitchen, an oak fired oven in a sparkling tile chimney and a bustling staff making fresh breads, handmade pastas and steaming cups of fresh ground coffee. And it is here Chef Barickman becomes truly creative with Italian and Mediterranean touches to fresh local seafood and regional produce that is rather innovative for Charleston's taste. From his all-day menu you may start with artichoke bottoms stuffed with herbed goat cheese, a salad of warm sea scallops with mango lime dressing or an oak roasted chicken pizza from the wood burning oven. For pasta lovers try the Carolina crab ravioli or Blossom's handmade linguine with white clam sauce. They will fire roast salmon, grill lamb loin chops and saute grouper fillets and combine them with the finest of imported staples and local produce. Dining in their walled courtyard or inside with oven aromas, both the cuisine and impeccable service prove that this Blossom Cafe did not fall far from the parent Magnolia tree.

Blossom Cafe Oven Roasted Salmon

2 6 oz salmon fillets
1 chopped onion
1/4 cup calamata olives
2 tblsps chopped parsley
2 tblsps chopped basil
1 tsp oregano
1 cup cherry tomatoes
Balsamic vinegar
olive oil
1 cup orzo pasta

Season salmon with salt & pepper & roast in wood burning oven, serving side up. Turn when 1/2 done & add onions. Simmer tomatoes in oil & vinegar with herbs till soft. Remove, add wine & butter to pan to make sauce. Cook orzo with herbs & mound on plates. Place salmon on top with onions, add tomatoes & pour sauce over. Garnish with parsley. Serves two.

MAGNOLIAS

185 East Bay Street (843) 577-7771 Major Credit Cards
Lunch $8 Dinner $16

If you had to describe the beauty, charm and fragrance of the Old South in a word it would be magnolias. And if you had to select one restaurant that epitomized the gentility, artistry and flavors of southern living, that word too would be Magnolias. It is perhaps the most celebrated dining spot in Charleston, serving southern contemporary cuisine in an antebellum ambiance that is both elegant and comfortable. There are areas to complement any mood or taste, from a bistro style "Chef's Room" to "The Gallery" for quiet intimate dining surrounded by gorgeous Rod Goebel paintings. However, it is the artistry of Chef Donald Barickman who reinvented southern cooking that makes Magnolias so popular. He has given new meaning to grits served with spicy shrimp or grilled salmon, with sauteed chicken or blackened green tomatoes. His Down South eggrolls, game hen or black grouper are served with fresh collards or greens as mouth watering as his carpetbagger filet with fried oysters or his veal meatloaf. For a true taste of the culinary renaissance in Charleston, one must dine at this Uptown, Down South, Magnolias!

Magnolias Down South Egg Rolls

1 lb chicken breasts
1 cup small strips of Tasso
2 cups collard greens
8 egg roll wrappers
2 cups julienned onion
2 tblsps olive oil
1-1/2 tblsps minced garlic
cornstarch & water mix

Cut skinned & boneless chicken breasts into thin strips & saute in olive oil with onions & garlic for 5 minutes until done. Cook collard greens, drain well, add to fry pan & heat thru. Let cool & drain well. Place 3/4 cup mixture on each wrapper, brush edges with cornstarch mix, fold ends, roll up & seal. Deep fat fry in Canola oil until golden crisp. Cut on diagonal & stand on plate. Serve with red pepper sauce, spicy mustard & peach chutney. Makes 8 egg rolls.

SARACEN

141 East Bay Street (843) 723-6242 Major Credit Cards
Dinner $11 Closed Sunday & Monday

The architecture of Saracen is regarded as the most distinctive in the city, the cuisine is certainly as unique and tasteful and Charlie Farrell is one of the most intriguing restaurateurs you will meet anywhere. She spent years as a chef in Paris and on private yachts cruising the Mediterranean, and that influence shows in the Turkish, Moorish decor and in her menu that is extraordinary by design. Her blue cheese fondue appetizer, Thai glazed lamb loin in a spicy black bean sauce or her curry toasted Mahi-Mahi defy the mundane as does her shrimp and grits with tomatoes, tarragon and a touch of sherry. The menu changes seasonally but her veal meatloaf with mashed potatoes du jour and the grilled beef tenderloin with green peppercorn bearnaise and portobello fritters are not to be missed. Nor is "Charlie's Little Bar" upstairs that is the hopping spot for late night Charlestonians. It has been hailed by guests as "Fabulous food in an exquisite setting...A five-star restaurant...and Mystical"! Dining at Saracen is a rare, romantic and delicious experience... thanks to Charlie Farrell!

Beef Tenderloin w/ Green Peppercorn Bearnaise

2 8 oz beef filets
2 egg yolks
1 tblsp white wine vinegar
4 oz clarified butter
2 tsps fresh tarragon
1 tblsp green peppercorns
1 tblsp lemon juice
1 cup mashed potatoes
1/4 cup balsamic glaze
2 portobello fritters

Season beef filet with salt & pepper to taste & grill to desired doneness.
For sauce, whisk yolks in double boiler with vinegar till foamy. Drizzle in butter until thick, remove & whisk in remaining ingredients.
Spoon mashed potatoes on plate & top with filet. Spoon bearnaise over & drizzle with balsamic glaze.
Garnish with portobello fritter & rosemary sprig.
Serves two.

McCRADY'S TAVERN

2 Unity Alley (843) 577-0025 Closed Saturday Lunch & Sunday
Lunch $7 Dinner $15 Major Credit Cards

Almost hidden down cobblestoned Unity Alley is the most historic tavern in all of Charleston. McCrady's has been a tradition for those who enjoy fine dining since 1778, including a well documented dinner for George Washington some 200 years ago. Today, with its warm brick walls, fireplace bar, and arched doorways it is like dining back in time, with the exception of the contemporary cuisine created by Chef Jose de Anacleto. Trained in France from age 16, Jose came to the States and opened Restaurant Million with a fresh approach to classic French dining. At McCrady's his talents have gone a step further with innovative American menus featuring fresh seafood, pasta and huge steaks. T-bones or Porterhouse of a pound or more with fried mashed potatoes are modestly priced as is his grilled salmon, pan seared Tilapia and curried scallops. His sauteed shrimp over yellow grits or the grouper with cabbage are Lowcountry with a French flair that makes them exceptional. Between his French Million and American McCrady's, Jose has revolutionized Charleston's dining.

Potato Gnocchi w/ Wild Mushrooms

2 lb baking potatoes
12 oz flour
3-1/2 oz butter, softened
3-1/2 oz romano cheese
1 whole egg
salt & pepper
1 cup marinara sauce
mixed wild mushrooms & green peas for garnish

Peel & cook potatoes al dente & drain well. Grind through small disk. Add flour, butter, cheese, egg & salt & pepper to taste. Mix well until just incorporated. Scoop into 1-1/2 oz balls & refrigerate until cold. Roll into 2-1/2 inch cylinders & refrigerate 1 hour. Cook in boiling water until gnocchi's float. Pour marinara sauce into bowls & arrange gnocchi over. Garnish with sauteed mushrooms, green peas & fried beet slices. Serves six.

82 QUEEN

82 Queen Street (843) 723-7591 Major Credit Cards
Lunch $8 Dinner $17

82 Queen actually refers to their address in the heart of the downtown historic district, but for 15 years this culinary landmark has been pleasing the royal families of Charleston with some of the best Low Country cuisine found in the region. In three separate buildings, this preeminent restaurant boasts seven distinctive dining rooms and three garden areas where one may dine under blooming camellias and stately palmetto trees. These intimate and romantic settings are the perfect backdrop for the cuisines of Chef Stephen Kish. His Plantation duck with Grand Marnier glaze, McClellanville crabcakes or his Southern Comfort BBQ shrimp over grits set a standard for fine regional cooking. To celebrate their 15th Anniversary, Steve's menu still features his award winning She Crab Soup and other favorites but with added new items such as Fried Green Tomatoes and Crawfish and Shrimp Jambalaya along with two signature wines bottled exclusively for 82 Queen. Mimosas and magnolias, authentic Low Country cuisine, fine wines and service, make dining at 82 Queen an ideal Southern experience.

BBQ Shrimp & Grits

24 med shrimp, cleaned
1/4 lb bacon, diced
1 cup red onion, diced fine
1/2 cup each red & green pepper, diced fine
24 oz ketchup
1/2 cup brown sugar
2 oz Southern Comfort
salt & pepper to taste
2 cups instant grits

For BBQ sauce:
Cook bacon until 3/4 done. Add onion & peppers & saute until done. Flame with Southern Comfort. Add ketchup & sugar & simmer 10 minutes. Let cool. Cook grits in 1 quart water, 1 cup heavy cream & 1/4 lb of butter. Saute or poach shrimp in butter until almost done. Place in BBQ sauce & simmer 1 minute. Arrange shrimp over grits & garnish with chopped scallions. Serves two.

CAROLINA'S

10 Exchange Street (843) 724-3800 Major Credit Cards
Dinner $11

A beautiful life-size portrait of Carolina's owner, Nancy Snowden, graces one wall and sets an elegant yet casual stage for one of Charleston's most elite restaurants. The dining rooms are an eclectic mix of mirrors and glass, tile and steel and classic columns, oil paintings and huge vases of flowers. The cuisines created at Carolina's by Executive Chef Rose Durden are as exquisite as the settings. Influenced by her Asian heritage, Rose adds spice to lowcountry fare with her unique assortment of chutneys, relishes, sauces, jams and syrups. Golden grits with grilled Andouille sausage and Rose's Pepper Jam, lamb tenderloin with her Eggplant and Sun-dried Tomato Chutney or sauteed shrimp with a touch of her Hot Habanero Sauce are delicious samplings that make dining here unforgettable. For milder tastes her Tropical Fruit Chutney is superb over lamb, grouper, quail and their mixed seafood grill. Carolina Rose products are available as well as her catering services for private functions. But for the epicurean or anyone with a passion for food, Carolina's will be one of Charleston's most delicious memories!

Charleston Seafood Pot

8 oz salmon
8 oz dolphin
6 oz shrimp
2 oz raspberry sauce
8 oz butter
2 tblsps chopped shallots
1/2 cup white wine
salt & pepper to taste

Season the fish, shrimp & scallops with salt and pepper. Brush thoroughly with melted butter and grill for three minutes on each side. Do not overcook. Meanwhile, to make butter sauce, combine wine & shallots in heavy sauce pan & reduce until little wine remains. Add raspberry sauce & butter & stir briskly until mixture thickens. Arrange fish on plates, top with shrimp & scallops, pour sauce over & serve with mixed vegetables. Serves two.

SOUTHEND Brewery & Smokehouse

161 East Bay Street (843) 853-4677 Major Credit Cards
Lunch $6 Dinner $11

The building that warehoused cotton and grain back in the 1800's is today filled with the aromas of brewing hops, a wood burning oven, apple cobbler, pizzas and barbecued ribs and chicken. It is also filled daily with patrons who have discovered this unique restaurant can satisfy both your hunger and thirst with an incredibly diverse menu and a dozen freshly brewed beers. The Southend Brewery & Smokehouse has three floors for dining, live entertainment, banquet facilities and a harbor-view bar for TV, billiards and cigars. But it's their award winning ales and beers and large portions of great food prepared in an open kitchen that makes this place so popular. The chef's daily menu may offer corn chowder soup, a Charleston oyster bake or a hardwood grilled NY strip, while their "Smokehouse Brew-B-Que" specials of beef brisket, ale steamed sausage, baby back ribs, pork chops, tenderloins, fish and chicken are always featured. Between the chefs, brewmeisters and smokemeister, they create over 50 delicious items and ales, served in delightful surroundings that are bound to please both palate and purse.

BBQ Beef Brisket w/ Smoked Bacon Mashed Potatoes

5 lb beef brisket
cayenne pepper
4 cloves fresh garlic
1 tsp cumin
2 lbs potatoes
6 slices smoked bacon
2 tblsps roasted garlic
1/2 pint sour cream
4 tblsps butter
salt & pepper

Dry rub both sides of brisket with mix of cayenne pepper, crushed fresh garlic cloves, cumin, salt & pepper. Place brisket in smoker fatty side up & cook 12 hours at 200 degrees until tender. Peel & boil potatoes until soft. Mash together with roasted garlic, sour cream, cooked bacon slices, butter, salt & pepper to taste & serve with sliced brisket & vegetables. Garnish with Southend BBQ sauce. Serves six.

BEAUMONT'S Cafe & Bar

12 Cumberland Street (843) 577-5500 Major Credit Cards
Lunch $8 Dinner $14

Of the many restaurants offering French menus, there are none more authentic than Beaumont's Cafe & Bar in historic Charleston. From their Tri-colors flying outside the door to chefs and owner, this casual provencal restaurant is as pure French as the Arc de Triumph. Owner Jean Marc Petin and his wife or mother welcome every guest with a fluent "Bon Jour", the French menus with English sub-titles are easily understood and their wait staff can recite daily specials bi-lingually. The cuisine, expertly presented by Chefs Gilg and Deslandes is typical of the French Provinces with lighter sauces, roasted vegetables, hearty soups, meats, fish and seafood. The terrine de campagne, a country pate, escargot stuffed in potato crusts or the oysters with hollandaise are delectable appetizers. Their Medaillons de lapin, Cuisses de Grenouilles, Canard a L'ail and Carre d'Agneau au Four are rabbit, frog legs, duck and rack of lamb, deliciously prepared as only the French know how. The casual ambiance, decor, an open courtyard and cigar-friendly bar, the fine wines and superb cuisine make Beaumont's a French Quarter classic!!!

Beaumont's Chocolate Supreme

2 cups unsweetened chocolate
1 cup dark sweet chocolate
3/4 cup unsalted butter
1 cup espresso
1 cup heavy cream
5 egg yolks
lady fingers
Grand Marnier

Place chocolate with butter in double boiler & heat until melted. Add espresso, heavy cream & egg yolks. Remove from heat, place in ice and mix by hand for 15 minutes. Mold pie pan with lady fingers drizzled with Grand Marnier. Pour chocolate mix into pan & chill 2 hours or overnight. Slice into wedges & serve upright on plate with vanilla cream & raspberry sauces. Garnish with strawberrys. Makes one pie.

PUSSER'S® LANDING

City Marina 17 Lockwood Drive (843) 853-1000 Major Credit Cards
Lunch $7 Dinner $13

Any visitor to the Virgin Islands knows that the name Pusser means not only a great rum but a family of fine waterfront restaurants specializing in seafood and Caribbean fare. All of Pusser's stateside locations, in Annapolis, Wrightsville Beach, Fort Lauderdale and Charleston provide the same warm ambiance, waterfront vistas and distinctive cuisine that originated on Tortola in the BVI's. Pusser's Landing, overlooking the City Marina in the beautifully restored historic old Rice Mill Building, provides a splendid harbor view. The menu offers varied items from fried green tomatoes or Carolina crab cakes, to jerk chicken with mango salsa or a Jamaican seafood pot. They are renowned for the Pusser's Rum Pain Killers and other island rum drinks as well as desserts like their mango souffle, mud pies and pan fried, honey bananas. Pusser's is equally famous for their Co. Stores which feature their prioprietary tropical and nautical clothing and unusual gifts and accessories from around the world. For a true taste and feel of the Caribbean, just dine and shop at any of Pusser's fine restaurants and Co. Stores.

Pan Seared Black & White Tuna

4 8 oz tuna fillets
black & white sesame seeds
clarified butter
1-1/2 lbs mixed vegetable: baby corn, snow peas, shredded green cabbage, sliced carrots, chopped celery & bokchoy, red & green peppers julienned, sliced mushrooms & broccoli flowrettes
4 tblsps stir fry sauce
wasabi sauce
1 lb cooked rice

Dredge tuna fillets in black & white sesame seeds & cook on griddle in claified butter on both sides to desired temperature. Meanwhile cook vegetable mix in wok with stir fry sauce until tender crisp. Place rice in center of plate & surround with vegetables. Top rice with tuna and spoon wasabi sauce over. Serves four.

ROSEBANK FARMS CAFE

Bohicket Marina 1886 Andell Bluff Seabrook Island (843) 768-1807
Lunch $6 Dinner $16 Major Credit Cards

The 100 acre Rosebank Farm and its owner, Sidi Limehouse, are considered institutions on Seabrook Island, offering fresh vegetables and flowers at their roadside stand for years. Sidi may also be credited for preserving the live oak trees that line the most beautiful roadway on this island which leads to his latest and perhaps best endeavor. Here you'll find his daughter Julie running the Rosebank Farms Cafe and serving the best low country cuisine imaginable. Her chef, Casey Taylor combines vegetables picked at Sidi's farm daily with seafood, meats and chicken for delicious dishes like veal chops and braised cabbage, or quail with sieva bean-mushroom demi and squash casserole. A grilled dolphin sandwich on rosemary bread, their fried green tomato and brie BLT, or the Blue plate lunch specials with an entree and two fresh vegetables are all about $7. For your grits fits, have them with crawfish, ham and shrimp or panfried with roasted duck. The cornmeal crusted catfish with Creole and mango chili sauce, or the chance to meet Sidi and Julie are worth any cruise or drive to Rosebank Farms and Cafe!

Catfish with Grits, Creole Sauce & Mango Chili Glaze

4 1 lb catfish, dressed
1 qt grits
1 ancho chile
1 chipotle
1 mango, peeled & cut
1/4 cup sugar
1/4 cup vinegar
2 garlic cloves, crushed
2 shallots, chopped
1/2 cup water
1 cup creole sauce

Score catfish with X's, dredge in cornmeal & deep fry until crispy done. Cook grits in milk with butter & salt till soft. For glaze, mix remaining ingredients & simmer on low heat for 20 mins, then puree. Arrange catfish on plates, top with glaze & serve with creole sauce, grits & squash. Garnish with rosemary sprigs. Serves four.

Beaufort *mm 537*

Like a sister city north, Beaufort, S.C. is one of those ideal ports of call for boaters sailing the Intracoastal Waterway as well as landside travelers looking for interesting places to visit. The ICW flows along the edge of town with a city marina and waterfront parks welcoming yachtsmen ashore. Walking maps from their Visitors Center or horse drawn carriage tours provide an introduction to blocks of historic landmarks, beautiful old homes and churches and tree lined streets where Hollywood tales like Forrest Gump and Prince of Tides were filmed. The downtown street is filled with art galleries, gift shops, antique stores and cafes and restaurants overlooking the waterfront. Your dining choices of these restaurants are from low country cooking to very sophisticated cuisine, served in converted banks, modern bistros or an elegant old riverfront plantation. Beaufort is a charming, delightful culinary find!

THE BANK GRILL & BAR

926 Bay Street (843) 522-8831 Major Credit Cards
Lunch $6 Dinner $12 Closed Sunday

The Beaufort Bank was only open for 10 years before the depression of 1926, but today this classic Beaux Arts building is cashing in as a thriving Grill & Bar on Beaufort's rejuvenated waterfront. Now operated by Brenda and Andy Biddle, they have retained a banking theme with a ledger size menu that offers a five page culinary checkbook. The beginning balance sheet lists 20 appetizers from an awesome onion and stuffed jalapeno peppers to oyster shooters. Shrimp comes with 7 flavors or on one of their healthy choice salads and one page is devoted to Bank burgers and super sandwiches from crab melts to peanut butter and jelly for junior investors. Black Angus steaks are charbroiled on lava rocks for a juicy taste you can bank on and the chef's crabcakes, lobster, stir frys and low country suppers will make your returns frequent. Liquid assets include luscious drinks and wines and your "teller" will serve delicious desserts as an ending balance. For excellent dining, ambiance and service, credit must go to Brenda and Andy for making The Bank Grill & Bar a culinary asset for Beaufort.

Greek Shrimp Feta

16 large shrimp
2 oz olive oil
2 tsps minced fresh garlic
3 tblsps diced tomatoes
15 whole black olives
2 tblsps chopped scallions
1/2 cup feta cheese
1 tblsp sherry
parmesan cheese
1 lb angel hair pasta
dash of oregano, thyme, basil & marjoram

Peel and devein shrimp and saute in olive oil until pink. Add tomatoes, scallions, olives and sherry and saute until hot. Season with spices and simmer for about 2 minutes. Meanwhile cook pasta al dente, drain and arrange on plate or large pasta bowl. Spoon shrimp mixture over pasta and garnish with parmesan cheese. Serves two.

PLUMS Waterfront Cafe

904-1/2 Bay Street (843) 525-1946 VISA MC DISC
Lunch $5 Dinner $12

Tucked in behind two Bay Street shops with panoramic views of the river and a waterfront park, this is one cafe visitors to Beaufort should not overlook. Plums is small with cafe chairs, fresh flowers and colorful prints, but the secret here is that you pay for good food instead of decor. And the cuisine created in their tiny kitchen by owner Lantz Price and chef Will Mclenagan is close to phenomenal. They have a repertoire of 150 soups from clam Florentine to a Portuguese stew. Greek, Spanish and Mediterranean influences are only a part of an international menu that includes New Zealand lamb, French Quarter shrimp, Chilean salmon, Cuban nachos , N'Awlins barbeque, Sante Fe chicken and Montego Bay pork. Saga Bleu, Crawfish Ya Ya and Fruta di Mare are fantastic pasta dishes with homemade sauces and seafood. In fact everything is made fresh and nothing is fried. They even have their own ice cream factory with 8 flavors du jour including one designed by Barbara Streisand called Prince Of Tides. For beer lovers there's a 40 something selection of micro brews but Plums forte is just good, good food !

Fruta di Mare

24 fresh mussels
16 fresh scallops
16 fresh topneck clams
16 fresh shrimp, cleaned
2 tblsps olive oil
1/4 cup white wine
marinara sauce

To make marinara: Saute chopped onion & 2 celery stalks in olive oil till clear. Add chopped garlic cloves & saute till golden brown. Add 4 cans chopped tomatoes, 8 oz chicken stock, 1/4 cup fresh basil & 1 tblsp sugar. Bring to a boil & simmer 1 hour. Salt to taste. Saute scallops & shrimp in olive oil, searing on both sides for 2 mins. Add clams, mussels & wine & steam till shellfish open. Add half of marinara sauce & simmer till done. Pour into bowl, top with marinara & garnish with parsley & basil leaves. Serves four.

LA SIRENA

822 Bay Street (843) 524-2500 Major Credit Cards
Lunch $7 Dinner $13

David LeBoutillier is actually a consultant whose menus and restaurant designs were selected as the best in the U.S. by James Beard and Esquire. But David recently turned this talent to his own restaurant, La Sirena, and made it a new trend setter for sophisticated dining in Beaufort. Based on the small cafes found in old fishing villages along the Italian Riviera, La Sirena's menu features antipasti of stuffed mussels "Ligurian style", grilled scallops wrapped in pancetta, beef carpaccio and zuppa di giorno. Their pasta dishes may be ordered in whole or half portions with seafood, chicken or Italian sausage and pesto or light tomato sauces. Typical of the "rustic cuisine" of Tuscany, the fresh salmon, mahi-mahi, tuna and steaks are cooked over a wood fired grill as is the rack of lamb with an herb, garlic crust that is sensational. To complement the cuisine they offer light wines of California and Italy, served by the glass from new labels weekly. La Sirena means a siren of the sea, a mythical mermaid with an alluring call. David's restaurant lives up to the name with its provocative cuisine, exceptional service and their savoir faire ambiance.

La Sirena Crusted Rack of Lamb

2 4 chop racks of lamb
Sam Adams beer
grapefruit juice
bay leaves
peppercorns
1 tblsp olive oil
4 garlic cloves
grated parmesan cheese
bread crumbs
herb mix of oregano, thyme & rosemary

Marinate lamb in mix of next four ingredients for 24 hours. Remove & sear off lamb in skillet to seal in juices. Prepare mixture of minced garlic, parmesan cheese, bread crumbs, thyme, oregano, rosemary and olive oil. Coat each rack with thick crust of herb mixture & finish on wood grill. Slice chops & arrange on plate with roasted root vegetables. Garnish with rosemary. Serves two.

WHITEHALL PLANTATION

27 Whitehall Drive (843) 521-1700 Closed Sunday Dinner & Mondays
Lunch $8 Dinner $18 AE VISA MC

There are few chefs anywhere that have as many awards and accolades as Sture Anderson, owner of Whitehall Plantation. Formally of Sweden, he served on the USA Culinary Team that took the Grand Prize worldwide, and has been honored by the American Academy of Chefs. He created the culinary art for 28 movies and TV shows as studio chef in Los Angeles for years. Sture was the executive chef in Pinehurst, Hilton Head and at Bluebeard's Castle in the Virgin Islands before opening his restaurant in one of Beaufort's oldest landmarks. It is like stepping back in time to dine in a surrounding of landscaped gardens with 400 year old live oaks while watching magnificent sunsets over the Beaufort River. Chef Anderson completes the illusion of life on a plantation with presentations of Lobster Savannah, Rack of Lamb prepared tableside, Low Country Crab Cakes, Shrimp Beaufort as well as home made Southern Pecan Pie. With his wife Beverly, Chef Sture makes Whitehall Plantation the ideal setting for private parties, weddings, receptions and for truly unique, fine dining experiences!

Whitehall Plantation Lobster "Arc En Ciel"

2 1-1/4 lb lobsters
2 cups julienned carrots, zuccinii & yellow squash
butter
1/2 cup black bean ragou
2 oz cilantro
1/2 cup each red & green pepper coulis

Boil or steam lobsters until just done. Remove claw & tail meat. Save heads, legs & fan tail shells. Meanwhile lightly saute vegetables in butter & mold in 3" savarin. Unmold onto center of plate & pour red & green coulis around. Top vegetable with black bean ragou flavored with cilantro. Split lobster tail meat & arrange on plate with claw meat and lobster shells & legs. Serves two.

OLD OYSTER FACTORY

On Broad Creek 101 Marshland Road (843) 681-6040
Dinner $15 Major Credit Cards

On this site in 1925, the original cannery harvested oysters from over 1700 acres of surrounding creeks and wetlands and shipped them to buyers from Savannah to Charleston. Today The Old Oyster Factory still harvests Hilton Head oysters from beds outside its doors, but serves them to patrons who come here to dine at one of the island's finest seafood and steakhouse restaurants. Fresh from the waters one can enjoy delicious oysters, raw, fried or served Provencale, Rockefeller, Savannah or as an Oyster Caesar Salad. Owner/chef Franz Auer is an artist with fresh local lobster, Mahi Mahi, grouper, swordfish, scallops and shrimp, delivered daily from work boats docked at their back door. Yet he is equally talented with his chargrilled breast of chicken with herb butter, pastas and his hand trimmed steaks, from filet mignon with bernaise to a 16 oz New York strip. Overlooking the marshlands and oyster beds of Broad Creek, The Old Oyster Factory is the ideal escape from the madding crowds where guests may relax, watch a beautiful sunset while savoring creations of a masterful chef and host!

Old Oyster Factory Seafood Gumbo

16 clams
2 small lobsters
32 mussels
3 lb can diced tomatoes
8 oz tomato paste
1 onion, chopped
1 each red, yellow & green peppers, diced
2 jalapeno peppers, sliced
1 tsp each oregano, thyme & basil leaves
2 tblsps chopped garlic
1/2 tsp white pepper
1 lb sliced okra
1 tsp chopped parsley
1 gallon fish stock

Steam lobsters, mussels & clams until just done. Meanwhile saute peppers & onion in oil, add tomatoes & paste & saute 3 minutes. Add remaining ingredients, bring to a boil, then simmer 1/2 hour. Pour sauce into bowls & add lobster pieces, clams & mussels.
Serves 8 to 10.

TWO ELEVEN PARK

211 Park Plaza (843) 686-5212 Major Credit Cards
Dinner $12 Closed Sunday

On any perfectly manicured island like Hilton Head it is always a pleasure to find a restaurant serving a unique variety of cuisine with a great selection of wines in a casual, let-your-hair-down, laid back atmosphere. The Two Eleven Wine Bar & Bistro was styled by owner, Bill Cubbage, a real South Carolinian, to be all that and more. For starters, as a former wine purveyor, he is an expert on the more than 200 labels available in his cellar. Bill then teamed up with Richard Canestrari, a culinary grad whose Southern Fusion cooking is a mix of low country traditions with some Mexican, Italian and Thai influences. Nightly chef specials may feature a crusted rack of lamb, a trio of seafood over linguine with a Thai peanut sauce or grilled quail over Savannah red rice, spicy andouille sausage, grilled shrimp and collard greens. There are crab grit cakes, low country paella, a rasta pasta, gourmet pizzas du jour and a tuna, tuna, tuna sushi. An intriguing mural covers one wall depicting some famous and perhaps infamous patrons dining at Two Eleven Park. Regardless of one's status, this is one fun filled place to dine!

Thai Seafood Trio

4 fresh softshell crabs
4 jumbo shrimp
4 5 oz lobster tails
olive oil
linguine cooked al dente

For Thai sauce: Combine 1 cup peanut butter, 2 cups fish stock, 1/4 cup soy sauce, 4 chopped green onions & 1 tblsp chopped garlic. Bring to boil & simmer 15 mins till creamy. For Chili sauce: Combine 1 tblsp red pepper flakes, 2 jars apricot jelly, 2 tblsps minced garlic, 1 cup rice vinegar & I cup chopped cilantro. Bring to boil & simmer 20 mins. Pan saute seafood in olive oil till just done & toss with hot chili sauce. Mix pasta with Thai sauce and mound on plate. Top with seafood & garnish with rice noodles & chopped green onions. Serves two.

ICW Bonus Recipes

French Quarter Duck A L'Orange

1 4 to 5 lb duckling
lemon juice
celery leaves & sliced onion
1-1/2 cups dry white wine
1 tblsp honey

Trim neck & wing tips of duckling . Rub cavity with lemon juice & add onion & celery leaves. Cook breast side up in 325° oven for 30 mins. Drain fat, add wine & cook 1-1/2 hrs basting every 20 mins. Brush with honey before last 15 mins. For sauce heat 1/2 cup sugar & 1 tblsp wine vinegar until sugar melts. Add juice of 2 oranges, 1/2 cup Grand Marnier & grated rind of an orange. Stir & cook 5 mins. Add juice from roasting pan & 1/4 cup of pre-cooked julienned orange peel. Split duck in half, pour sauce over & garnish with bing cherries & pineapple. Serves two.

Amory's Spicy Hollandaise Oysters

24 oysters in shells
1 cup flour
1 cup cornmeal
1 tblsp Old Bay
4 egg yolks
1/4 cup clarified butter
1 lemon
1 tblsp horseradish
1 tsp each, fresh basil, rosemary & parsley

Shuck oysters, save botom shell. Dredge oysters in mix of flour, cornmeal & Old Bay. Pan fry in hot peanut oil until golden brown on both sides. Meanwhile drizzle butter into egg yolks in double boiler while stirring. Add horseradish, lemon juice and herbs, chopped fine. Spoon tblsp Hollandaise in each shell & top with oysters. Garnish with lemon slices, greens & horseradish. Serves four.

Courtyard on Grove Chicken Janice with Lemon Dill Sauce

2 chicken breasts, trimmed
6 oz cream cheese
1 small white onion
2 tblsps lemon juice
2 cloves garlic, minced
1 tsp dill
1 tblsp white wine

Lightly pound breasts to even thickness. Blend cream cheese, minced onion, lemon juice, wine, garlic & dill. Mound 2 tblsps mixture on each breast & fold to cover. Lightly dust with flour, saute in olive oil until half done & finish in 350 degree oven for 7 to 9 minutes. For sauce: Combine 2 tblsps lemon juice, 2 tblsps white wine, 1 tsp dill & bring to a boil. Reduce heat, stir in 3 tblsps butter to thicken. Pour over breast & serve with rice & vegetables. Serves two.

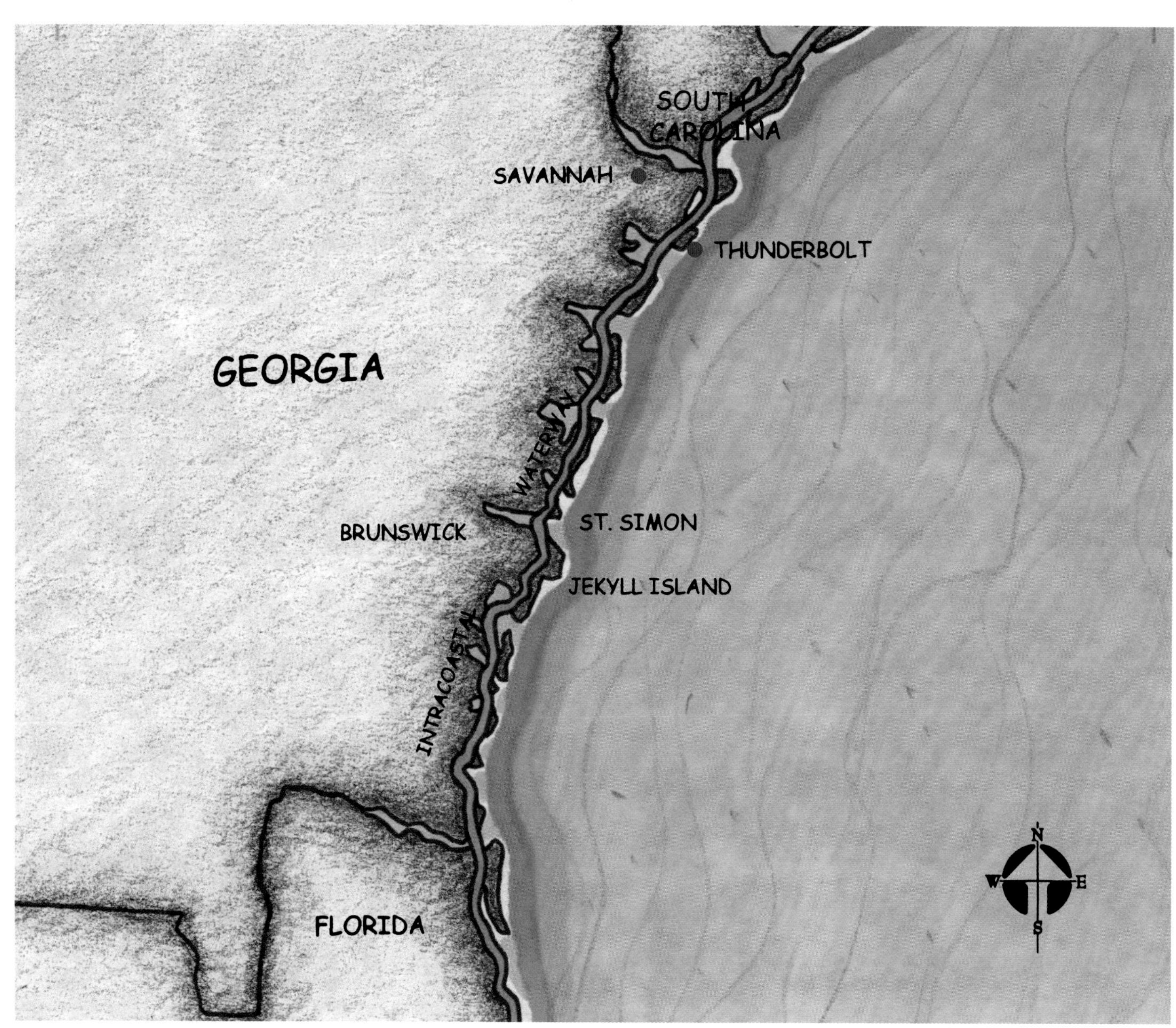
SOUTH
CAROLINA
SAVANNAH
THUNDERBOLT
GEORGIA
WATERWAY
ST. SIMON
BRUNSWICK
JEKYLL ISLAND
INTRACOASTAL
FLORIDA
N
W
E
S

GEORGIA mm 576 to 717

The Georgia shoreline is unlike any other Atlantic Coast state for it is a serpentine collection of wide sounds, rivers and creeks protected from the sea by a series of barrier islands. For nature lovers, these low lying wetlands are virtually undisturbed with miles of habitat for waterfowl and wildlife. Many of the barrier islands like St. Catherines are protected, while others including St. Simon and Jekyll have become luxury resort colonies with golf and tennis clubs and fashionable homes. Visitors are welcomed everywhere with historical tours and shopping in quaint coastal villages with Savannah as a main attraction. Boaters may tie up in Thunderbolt and bus to town in lieu of the eight mile trip upriver, but either by boat or car, this is one place you must visit to experience the lifestyle and enjoy the architecture and taste the cuisines of this charming southern city in Georgia.

Savannah mm 583

In Savannah, John Berendt's sensational best seller, *Midnight in the Garden of Good and Evil,* is simply called "The Book", for it is the best description you will ever read of the character and characters of this unique city in Georgia. Bus tours now feature the intriguing locations of "The Book" and bring to life this southern saga. But the history of Savannah predates this era by a few hundred years when General Oglethorpe designed its garden-like parks and streets to become America's first planned city. The 18th and 19th century homes and buildings are today a "living museum", displaying 260 years of history with splendid mansions and ancient cobblestone paths. Old cotton warehouses lining Water Street along the riverfront have been converted into shops and taverns, but the best restaurants found in Savannah and nearby Thunderbolt are the following almost hidden culinary jewels.

THE OLDE PINK HOUSE

Reynolds Square 23 Abercorn Street (912) 232-4286
Dinner $16 AE VISA MC

It was known as the Habersham House when first built in 1771, but the name changed when the soft native brick bled through the stucco walls, changing the color from white to Jamaican pink. Today this National Landmark that once housed a bank and Civil War Generals, is now home to The Olde Pink House Restaurant and Planters Tavern, where one dines in Savannah's only 18th century mansion. Lovingly restored to its original grandeur by Elizabeth, Donna and Kiara Balish, elegant rooms echo to the delight of guests dining by candlelight or having spirits by a fireplace in the lower Tavern. The cuisine is southern, but Chef Dan Kim, an avid fisherman, features fresh seafood in dishes of pan seared scallops with apple chutney, shrimp with country ham and grit cakes, or black grouper stuffed with blue crab. Duck, chicken and lamb are served with succulent sauces and superb wines stored in the old bank vaults. Dining in the Olde Pink House is like a walk through history where ghosts of the past fill ageless halls and magnificent rooms now used for private parties. It is a delicious blending of past and present.

Pan Seared Jumbo Sea Scallops with Apple Chutney

16 jumbo sea scallops
salt & pepper
1 Granny Smith apple
1/4 cup raisins
2 tblsps apple cider vinegar
2 tblsps sliced almonds
2 tblsps brown sugar
pinch each of curry powder, clove, cinnamon & nutmeg
1 tblsp chopped ginger

Lightly salt & pepper sea scallops & sear in clarified butter in hot, non-stick pan for two minutes on each side. For apple chutney: Peel & dice apple into small cubes. Combine with remaining ingredients & simmer over low heat until sticky consistency, stirring occasionally. Place scallops on plates with apple chutney & saffron beurre blanc. Serves four.

45 SOUTH

At The Pirates' House East Broad & Bay Street (912) 233-1881
Dinner $21 AE VISA MC Closed Sunday

45 South is one of the most elegant dining experiences one will find in all of Savannah. Recommended by Playboy, Southern Living and Food & Wine and a recipient of the Georgia Trend Gold Award, this restaurant is renowned for its ambiance, impeccable service and a cellar whose sommelier offers two separate wine lists. The cuisine is contemporary, featuring regional specialties with innovative creations by Executive Chef, Joseph Lemos. Appetizers of pan seared oysters in a potato nest, spring rolls of duck and pork or his grilled quail are delicious works of art as is the house cured salmon tartare with creme fraiche and caviar salad. His entrees may list a rack of Cervena venison, breast of pheasant, Sonoma rabbit or elk, wild boar and ostrich when available. Sauteed grouper is served with Israeli couscous, or truffle infused potatoes with the rack of lamb and white cheddar tasso grit cakes accompany the charred pork tenderloin. Private luncheons and complimentary valet parking are available. For an evening of exquisite dining, make your reservations ahead at this award winning 45 South.

Salmon Tartare with Creme Fraiche & Caviar

3 minced pearl onions
3 minced shallots
1 head minced garlic
16 oz cubed cured salmon
1 tblsp chopped chives
1 tblsp chopped baby dill
6 leaves cilantro, chopped
1 tblsp hazelnut oil
1/2 tblsp sesame oil
1 tsp fish sauce
1/2 tsp lemon juice
2 tblsps creme fraiche
Beluga & salmon caviar & crisp beet chips for garnish

Blanch shallots, garlic & pearl onions for 3 minutes. Combine with next 8 ingredients until moistened. Place mixture in ring mold & chill. Unmold onto plates & top with dash of creme fraiche. Garnish with Beluga & salmon caviar & crisp beet chips.
Serves two.

IL PASTICCIO

2 East Brougton Street (912) 231-8888 Major Credit Cards
Dinner $15

The translation of the name IL Pasticcio actually means "joyful chaos", and that is precisely what this restaurant is all about. From the cacophony of dishes and pans in their open kitchen mixed with classic opera to wine corks popping and the laughter of excited guests, the stage is set for a delightful dining experience. It is as authentic Italian as the owners, Pino, Dominique and Fabrizio Venetico, who have designed their restaurant and cuisine to create a feel and taste of Tuscany unique to Savannah. The menu created by the owners and chef Melissa Hunt features classic Italian fare from zuppa del giorno to homemade tortellini and fettucini. The grilled portobello, eggplant stuffed with goat cheese or roasted mussels from a wood fired oven are superb appetizers before entrees of salmone alla Griglia or filet mignon crusted with gorgonzola. Chef Hunt's slow roasted duck breast with a black cherry sauce is as artistic as it is delicious, like all of her nightly specials. IL Pasticcio has private rooms for catering, a new bar for late night snacks and an award winning cellar to satisfy any wine aficionado. Joyful chaos at its very best!

Duck Breast with Black Cherry Sauce & Saffron Risotto

2 10 oz duck breasts
4 oz wild cherry preserves
4 oz demi glace
1/2 cup Arborio rice
saffron in warm water
2 tblsps parmesan cheese
1/2 cup chopped parsley
2 tblsps butter
1/2 tsp chopped garlic

Combine preserves & demi & reduce 1/2. Coat breasts with reduction & roast skin side up in 350 degree oven until desired doneness. Meanwhile saute garlic in butter, add cooked rice & stir. Add saffron juice 1 tblsp at a time while stirring until desired consistency. Add parmesan, parsley & salt & pepper to taste. Mound risotto on plates, top with breasts & serve with garlic sauteed arugula & radicchio. Serves two.

TUBBY'S TANK HOUSE

2909 River Drive (912) 354-9040 AE VISA MC
Lunch $7 Dinner $13

If ever there was a place on the ICW where boaters can tie up and tank out on good food and a barrel of fun, it is here in Thunderbolt at Tubby's Tank House. The name says it all, for the owner added a few pounds testing his entire menu. One starts with Tubby's Teasers from calamari to Spanky's spuds and ends with pecan pie and other freshly baked Tubby Temptations. Owners Ray Clark, Ansley and Cham Williams carry on Tubby's traditions of catching and serving the freshest fish available, from tuna and wahoo to Mahi-Mahi, grouper and King Mackerel, all caught locally and on your plate within 24 hours. They buy shrimp right off the boats to ensure they are fresh in salads and fried or steamed. They offer steaks, chicken and burgers, but little can top their oyster roasts in winter outside by an open fire. The Thursday night parties in season are a sight to behold where 1500 guests dine and dance to live music in the parking lots and watch beautiful sunsets along the Waterway. They cater parties and fix takeout platters for home or yacht, but "tanking out" at Tubby's is a happening one must see!

Grilled Mahi with Pasta Primavera

2 8 oz Mahi-Mahi fillets
12 medium shrimp
12 sea scallops
2 tblsps butter
2 cups sliced yellow squash zucchini, broccoli & carrots
1 lb angel hair pasta, cooked al dente
1 tsp each: Old Bay, garlic powder, parsley, thyme & oregano
6 oz white wine

Grill Mahi-Mahi fillets on open flame, leaving grill marks on top. Meanwhile clean shrimp & saute with scallops in butter until half done. Add vegetables until tender crisp. Add wine & pasta & heat through. Add seasoning to taste. Mound pasta on plates & arrange seafood around. Top with Mahi-Mahi fillets & garnish with parsley, kale & lemon wedges. Serves two.

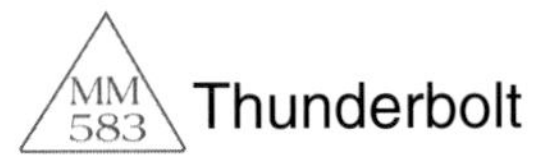

Thunderbolt

THE RIVER'S END

122 River Drive (912) 354-2973 Major Credit Cards
inner $15 Closed Sunday

verlooking the Intracoastal Waterway ıd the Palmer Johnson Marina is this ery special restaurant that has been erving Savannah since 1967. ocals and transient boaters ho have been coming to The iver's End for years know the uality of the cuisine and the nbiance never change, where veryone is made comfortable, essed in yachting gear or nery. Pianist Jack Rogers will member your favorite tune while owner ichael Strickland welcomes you as an d friend and chef Bryan prepares your ılmon fillet with a shredded potato crust or one of his many specialties. Their she crab soup with sherry, sauteed shrimp with cajun seasoning, scallops in a white cream sauce with spinach pasta or flounder stuffed with crab will satisfy any seafood lover. They have a special grill for broiling fresh fish, marinated in herbs and spices, basted in orange juice and topped with dill butter. And their steaks, rack of lamb, veal, chicken and duck entrees are equally superb. Featured in the N.Y. Times and Bon Appetit, with numerous awards and stars, The River's End is still your unpretentious, superb dining friend.

The River's End Salmon Thomas

4 8 oz salmon fillets
olive oil
salt & pepper to taste
2 sweet pototoes
2 cups white cream sauce
3 oz fresh basil
4 oz champagne
1/2 lb fresh spinach
3 tblsps butter

Peel sweet potatoes, slice thin & place in cold water. Brush salmon with oil, season to taste & grill 7-8 minutes until done. Meanwhile remove potato slices, deep fry till crispy, then drain. Saute spinach in butter 2-3 minutes until tender. Heat cream sauce & add basil & champagne. Bring to boil, stir & remove from heat. Center spinach on plates, top with salmon & ladle sauce over. Arrange potato slices on top. Serves four.

GEORGIA
FERNANDINA BEACH
JACKSONVILLE
DAYTONA BEACH
NEW SMYRNA
MERRITT ISLAND
ATLANTIC
OCEAN
MELBORNE
FLORIDA
VERO BEACH
STUART
W. PALM BEACH
PALM BEACH
GULF OF MEXICO
FT. LAUDERDALE
MIAMI
MIAMI BEACH
COCONUT GROVE
N
W
E
S
FLORIDA KEYS

FLORIDA mm 712 to 1094

From the relatively tranquil St. Mary's river on its Northern border to the megatropolis of Miami in the South, the state of Florida boasts some 380 miles of almost continuous beaches along a blue Atlantic coastline. But aside from its sunshine and tropical climes the state is also famous for its groves of citrus fruit, Disneyworld and even for raising cattle. Cruising down their Intracoastal Waterway, the scenery changes from wide open uncrowded sounds to a bustling "ditch" flowing between canyons of high rise condos and hotels. This busy aquatic highway is lined with luxurious homes and private communities and hundreds of vacation resorts, marinas and restaurants that cater to every imaginable taste and style. One may dine in splendor at 5-star resorts or crack crabs in a thatched Tiki bar at the water's edge. The following is a selection of Florida's very best.

Amelia Island/Fernandina *mm 716*

There is perhaps no better introduction to the State of Florida than Fernandina Beach on Amelia Island. It is the Northeasternmost corner of the state, just across the St. Mary's River from Georgia, making it an ideal port of call for yachts cruising the Atlantic or traveling the Intracoastal Waterway. The Fernandina Harbor Marina, adjoining the ICW, welcomes boaters with floating piers and professional dockhands, all within walking distance of a 50 block historic area lined with art galleries, smart shops, boutiques and Victorian inns. The Island provides miles of wide beaches with elegant resorts, golfing, tennis and sportfishing just offshore. This abundance of fresh fish and local seafood can be enjoyed in any of the following restaurants, prepared by masterful chefs and served in a warm and friendly atmosphere. Fernandina Beach is a delightful and delicious welcome to Florida!

BRETT'S WATERWAY CAFE

One South Front Street (904) 261-2660 AE VISA MC
Lunch $7 Dinner $17

With the fishing fleet docked just outside their doors, one would expect Brett's Waterway Cafe to prepare the freshest shrimp, fish and seafood found in historic Fernandina Beach. You would not be disappointed for their menu features items from crab cakes and scallops to a fresh catch of the day, as well as poultry and pastas, steaks and chops. It is also a shrimp lovers paradise, where only hours from the sea they are served fried or broiled with sun-dried tomato butter, boiled in beer with herbs and spices, on Caesar or Seafood Cobb salads or with a grilled filet. Other fantastic dishes by chef Robert Lannon include Cajun Pork Loin with Oysters, Fried Green Tomatoes with bearnaise and goat cheese, Bourbon St. Chicken saute, Lamb Chops with roasted peanuts and BBQ Scallops. The restaurant was featured on Southern Living's cover and has received numerous awards for the quality of food, decor and ambiance. Owners Brett Carter and Tip Fisher designed their Cafe to afford each guest spectacular views of the waterfront and sunsets while enjoying their outstanding cuisine, service and southern hospitality.

Barbecue Scallops over Polenta Cakes

24 sea scallops
2 tblsps butter
4 oz red onion
4 oz green bell pepper
4 oz red bell pepper
2 oz white wine
6 oz NC style BBQ sauce
6 oz cooked polenta

Cut all vegetables into match-stick size pieces, julienne style. Saute scallops and vegetables together in butter till tender crisp and almost done. Deglaze pan with white wine. Add BBQ sauce and simmer 3 to 5 minutes. Make two patty-style cakes from polenta & grill. Place cakes on plates and spoon scallop mixture over. Garnish with parsley and lemon wedges. Serves two.

THE MARINA RESTAURANT

101 Centre Street (904) 261-5310 VISA MC DC
Brkfst $2 Lunch $5 Dinner $8

The building housed the Nation's first Customs House, then Florida's oldest newspaper and finally in the early 1900's became the first fine dining restaurant in Fernandina Beach. The Marina Restaurant has been under the ownership of the Toundas family since 1966, and today Patricia carries on a tradition of serving great home style meals in a warm and cozy atmosphere. Diane Edmonds has been the head chef here for over 30 years and just one look at her menus explains why patrons line up at this "local's haunt". Her Old Favorites of Southern fried chicken, grilled liver and onions, baked lamb, veal, pork chops or country style steaks, served with a dozen choices of side dishes are just like Grandma made. But their specialty of the house is fresh local seafood, from oysters and crab to trout, flounder, scallops and shrimp, sauteed, stuffed, boiled, broiled, baked or fried to perfection and served in large portions. With a nautical theme The Marina Restaurant retains the flavor of the sea in its decor and cuisine and is so popular, locals and many city officials consider dining here a town hall meeting!

Shrimp & Scallops in Cream Sauce

1 lb scallops
1 lb shrimp
3 green onions, sliced thin
1/4 cup butter
1/4 tsp salt
1/4 cup dry white wine
2 tblsps cornstarch
1/2 cup whipping cream
1/4 lb grated parmesan
1 lb linguine

Saute onions in butter until tender. Add scallops & peeled & deveined shrimp. Add salt, stir & cook until almost done. Mix wine & cornstarch together & stir into seafood. Bring to a boil, reduce heat & stir in whipping cream. Add cheese & blend mixture with linguine, cooked al dente. Pour into bowl & serve with baked potato & hush puppies. Garnish with lemon wedges. Serves six.

1878 STEAK HOUSE

12 North 2nd Street (904) 261-4049 Major Credit Cards
Lunch $7 Dinner $15

In 1878 this building housed tons of tea, coffee, sugar and spices shipped in from around the world to local merchants. Over 100 years later it is still filled with the delectable aroma of food, now being served from plates rather than barrels. The old warehouse interior has been redecorated to reflect the Victorian period with paisley walls, antique sideboards, bentwood chairs and carpets for elegant dining upstairs, while the Brass Rail Lounge below is like a turn of the century saloon. Owner Johnie Davis and manager Bobby Brock have expanded the plans for her 1878 Steak House with a touch of New Orleans for patio dining and a menu featuring fresh seafood prepared just as expertly as their Certified Angus beef. Guests may now combine a steak cut to order tableside with snapper almondine, shrimp, lobster or flounder Fernandina. They offer a daily lunch buffet with meat and seafood, late night fare and live entertainment on weekends in addition to superb steaks and sauces. Those sea captains who lounged here a century ago would all love the company, cuisine and Johnie's dreams for 1878 Steak House.

Beef Tournedoes w/ Forrestierre Sauce

6 2 oz beef tenderloin medallions
garlic seasoning
salt & pepper
drawn butter
1/2 lb lump crab meat
Forrestierre sauce
Bernaise sauce

Season medallions with garlic, salt & pepper & sear off both sides in drawn butter in hot sautee pan until desired doneness. Add crab meat till heated. For Forrestierre sauce: Sautee chopped shallots & mushrooms in butter. Add vermouth & brandy, beef stock, cracked pepper, Heinz 57, dijon mustard & Worcestershire & reduce to a thick roux. Place tournedoes on plates, top with crab meat & blanched asparagus & pour sauces around. Serves two.

THE GOLDEN GROUPER CAFE

5 South 2nd Street (904) 261-0013 AE VISA MC DC
Lunch $7 Dinner $15 Seasonal Closings

As the name may imply, this small cafe in historic downtown Fernandina Beach features all kinds of seafood and fresh fish, but grouper just happens to be the favorite of young owners Brian & Susan McCarthy. After growing up in the family's Down Under Marina Restaurant on the ICW, they remodeled a former 1800's grocery store into a brightly Caribbean colored cafe and created a menu with cuisine so delicious they are packed daily for lunch and dinner. They offer steaks, chicken, super soups and salads, but the seafood from conch fritters to live Maine lobster is their thing. Many items like grilled red hot tuna, crab cakes or pepper shrimp can be ordered as appetizers or entrees which come with potatoes or rice, veggies and hush puppies. Their oysters, scallops and cumin crusted Mahi are sensational, but grouper, broiled, Cajun baked, as a chowder, grilled with creamy pesto or as spicy fingers is why they named it Golden. Their same seafood source for 17 years assures consistent, fresh quality for every dish, but it's their magical kitchen that makes The Golden Grouper Cafe a winner on Amelia Island!

Spicy Grouper Fingers

2 lbs grouper fillets
self rising flour
peanut oil
1-1/2 tblsps paprika
1/2 tblsp cayenne pepper
1/2 tblsp black pepper
3/4 tblsp lemon pepper
1/4 tblsp garlic salt

Remove all bones from grouper fillets & cut into 1/2 inch thick strips. Roll strips in spice mixture of last 5 ingredients & then in flour. Deep fry in 350 degree peanut oil until medium brown, about 3 to 4 minutes. Serve with rice cooked in chicken broth with chopped celery, carrot, broccoli, red onion & red & yellow pepper & season mix of 2 oz parsley, pinch of basil & salt & oregano, 1/4 tsp garlic salt, 2 tblsps margarine & 1/2 oz dijon mustard. Serves four.

CAFE ATLANTIS

22 South 4th Street (904) 277-0042 Major Credit Cards
Dinner $18

The cuisine of Cafe Atlantis is as varied as the location of that Atlantis lost off the coast of Greece, in the Caribbean, South America or in the South Pacific. It is rare to find a menu that has Middle Eastern Tabbouleh salad as well as Southwestern oysters gratinee, Ginger-soy glazed salmon with Asian greens or Jamaican jerk chicken with a tropical salsa. Yet, they are but a few of the dishes that owner and chef Brian Batsel recreates from his world travels as a former naval officer and graduate of L'Academie de Cuisine. Pursuing his love of cooking he designed Cafe Atlantis small for personal attention to each guest, built a vegetable and herb garden for patio dining and fresh produce for his kitchen and kept the wine and entree prices moderate as an exceptional value for superb dining. As the nautical name suggests they feature fresh fish and seafood but offer venison, lamb, veal and quail, all simply prepared with delicious sauces, soups and salads. There is a casual island ambiance and decor styled by Brian's wife, Tanis, that sets the stage for an evening of exceptional dining. We all hope this Atlantis never becomes lost!

Grilled Tuna with Spicy Fruit Salsa

4 6 oz tuna steaks
1/3 cup extra virgin olive oil
grated zest of 1 lime
1 tblsp chopped cilantro
2 tsps cracked black pepper
1 tsp salt

Coat tuna steaks with mix of cilantro, olive oil, lime zest & pepper & refrigerate.
For salsa: Dice 1 mango & 1/2 fresh pineapple into small cubes. Finely dice 1 red pepper & finely chop 1 habanero pepper with care. Mix all together with 1 cup diced Jicama root, juice of 1 lime, 2 tblsps chopped cilantro, 1 tsp sugar, 1/2 tsp salt & 1 tblsp rice vinegar. Set aside for 1/2 hour. Salt steaks & grill 3-4 minutes per side until medium rare. Serve with salsa, sauteed vegetables & rice. Garnish with cilantro sprig & star fruit. Serves four

HORIZONS

Corner of 8th & Ash Streets (904) 321-2430 Closed Sunday
Dinner $15 AE VISA MC

After years as one of Ritz Carlton's top women chefs, Courtney Thompson returned to Amelia Island, and with her mother Beebe, designed and opened her own restaurant, Horizons.
It was bestowed a Five Star rating and named "one of the top 25 restaurants on the First Coast" with a menu described as "nothing short of spectacular". All of these accolades are well deserved, for Chef Courtney's passion for cooking is evident in every dish from Tequila Dill Gravlax to her Pecan Pesto crusted Rack of Lamb. Elegant dining rooms with hues of navy and taupe and white linen tablecloths are the perfect settings for an evening of romantic dining or large catered parties. Her menu changes with the seasons and her creativity, but offers five specials nightly from fresh salmon, grouper or stuffed veal chops to duck breast. Everything is freshly made; soups, dressings and pastas, with homemade breads and delicious desserts baked in-house daily. This talented mother and daughter team make Horizons ideal for discriminating gourmets to enjoy excellent continental cuisine in a casual, refined ambiance.

Tequila Dill Gravlax

3 lbs fresh salmon
olive oil & fresh herbs
1 bunch fresh dill, chopped
1 tsp horseradish
4 tblsps sour cream
2 tblsps lime juice
1/2 shallot, minced
1/2 clove garlic, minced

Marinate salmon 24 hours in mix of oil, basil, thyme, rosemary & cracked black pepper. Place salmon on cookie sheet & slow smoke in bottom of 350 degree oven over tequila soaked hickory chips 4 to 6 hours.
Meanwhile for sauce:
Whisk together dill, sour cream, horseradish, lime juice, shallots & garlic. Chill for 1 hour.
Spoon sauce on plates & arrange salmon over. Serve with mixed baby greens & garnish with dry parsley. Serves four.

MARKER 32

14549 Beach Blvd.   (904) 223-1534   AE VISA MC
Dinner $15

As an international exchange student, Ben Groshell traveled and sampled the cuisine of Sweden, Portugal, Spain and Mexico and after graduating from The Culinary Institute of America, he added Polynesian cuisine to his skills and passion for cooking. Now as chef and owner of Marker 32, his menu still reflects an appreciation of the world's culinary arts by combining unique sauces and chutneys with fresh local seafood, meats, poultry and game. Patrons to this upscale, yet casual restaurant, are treated to tranquil views along the Intracoastal Waterway while enjoying seafood ceviche or duck wonton appetizers and entrees of grilled marinated quail or pan seared scallops and calamari over homemade pastas. They staff at least three CIA graduates, including Ben's brother Daniel who oversees the impeccable service and extensive wine list, and a pastry chef that produces fresh bread daily and incredible desserts from Amaretto Brulee to a Wild Banana Cheesecake with a peanut crust. Within sight of the ICW, Marker 32 is an absolute gem of a restaurant that every yachtsman and true gourmet must visit.

Santa Cruz Ceviche

1 lb shrimp
1 lb scallops, quartered
4 clams & 4 mussels
1 octopus tentacle
1 red, 1 yellow & 1 green pepper, diced small
1 small tomato, diced
1 small red onion, diced
handful fresh cilantro, chopped fine
juice of 3 lemons & 3 limes
dash of Tabasco
salt & pepper to taste
flour tortilla chips
vegetable oil

Peel & devein shrimp. Poach octopus in boiling water & cut apart. Steam clams & mussels & combine with all seafood. Marinate in lemon & lime juice for 24 hours. Combine peppers, cilantro, tomato & onion & add to marinade with salt, pepper & Tabasco before serving. Sprinkle chips with cumin & deep fry till crisp. Serves four.

Central Florida *mm 830 to 984*

With the exception of the restricted area of the sprawling Kennedy Space Center at Cape Canaveral, the Central Coast of Florida offers another 150 miles of gorgeous beaches for sunning, swimming and watching American astronauts being rocketed in orbit. It surely contains the most entertaining section of the state from NASCAR racing and Harley-Davis mania at Daytona Beach, to great off-shore fishing out of the St. Lucie Inlet at Stuart and the world famous Disney complex is just a short drive inland at Orlando. A narrow strip of land between the Intracoastal Waterway and the Atlantic is dotted with oceanfront homes and beach communities like Merritt Island, New Smyrna, Melbourne and Vero. It is also lined with these excellent restaurants featuring fresh local seafood, Continental and Caribbean cuisines where diners enjoy views of cruising yachts and the rockets red glare!

THE ST. REGIS

509 Seabreeze Blvd. (850) 252-8743 Closed Sunday & Monady
Lunch $8 Dinner $19 Major Credit Cards

Guests at the Regis de Montpellier Inn back in 1886 were so impressed with the accommodations and fine cuisine, they renamed their French host, "St. Regis". Today this historic old St. Regis house still offers their patrons exquisite cuisine, wonderful service and the same quaint atmosphere as was enjoyed over 100 years ago. It is like visiting a friend's home in the South of France with a veranda, patio bar and six beautifully decorated rooms for intimate dining, casual lunches or private catered parties. As owners, Constance and Henry White retained that European ambiance with fresh flowers, a grand piano and menus that feature both American and Continental cuisines and wines. Chicken Oslo with Swiss cheese and smoked salmon, boneless Duck A L'Orange or a Filet Au Poivre with green peppercorn sauce are favorites by chef Clara Hanson, who also bakes crispy French breads and desserts to die for. Her homemade soups and pastas, like the Shrimp and Scallop Martinique, are all prepared fresh daily and served with incredibly delicious light sauces. The spirit of St. Regis can be proud his dreams are still alive today!

St. Regis Shrimp Martinque w/ Pasta

1 lb jumbo shrimp
1 red, 1 yellow & 1 green pepper, julienned
1/4 tsp crushed red pepper
3 tblsps extra virgin olive oil
1 tblsp roasted garlic
2 tblsps key lime juice
1/4 cup white wine
1/4 cup gold rum
1/2 cup sundried tomatoes
1/4 cup diced green onions
2 tblsps butter
1 lb cooked linguine

Saute peppers in olive oil until half done. Add peeled & deveined shrimp, wine, garlic, red pepper, rum, lime juice & rehydrated sundried tomatoes. Simmer until shrimp are just done. Swirl in butter & toss with pasta, cooked al dente. Arrange shrimp & peppers on top & garnish with basil & parsley. Serves two.

SWEETWATER'S

3633 Halifax Drive (904) 761-6724 Major Credit Cards
Lunch $6 Dinner $10

As new owners in 1982, Barbara and Al Gaskill took this old waterfront restaurant with a cavernous interior and completely remodeled it into one of the most unique and appealing dining establishments in Port Orange. By dividing wide open spaces with a tropical jungle of trees and flowering plants, they created privacy and romantic settings with beautiful views of the ICW for hundreds of dining guests. While specializing in seafood, they have revamped their menus to include choices from fried alligator and frog legs to a 20 ounce T-bone, BBQ ribs, chicken, pastas and super salads and sinful desserts. It offers an International variety of cuisine like lobster from Canada, Denmark and Maine, Alaskan salmon, Boston scrod or Southern flounder, Jamaican, Malibu and Cajun chicken or local shrimp prepared a half dozen ways. Then consider homemade N.Y. style cheesecake, Key lime pie, a Black Forest trifle with only 3 fat grams and Espresso or Cappuccino to top off an exceptional dining experience. In spite of its size and popularity, their service is prompt, warm and personal, making Sweetwater's a rare treat indeed!

Linguine with Shrimp & Tomatoes

1 lb med shrimp, peeled
6 oz olive oil
2 oz basil leaves, torn
1/4 tsp salt
1/4 tsp white pepper
4 garlic cloves, chopped
4 green onions, sliced
1 cup diced plum tomatoes
1 lb linguine

Saute garlic & torn basil leaves in olive oil until basil is limp. Add shrimp & saute until shrimp are just pink. Add onions & tomatoes & saute until shrimp are just done. Season with salt & pepper & toss to coat. Meanwhile cook pasta al dente & drain. Divide into four bowls & spoon shrimp mixture over. Garnish dishes with fresh grated parmesan cheese & finely chopped parsley.
Serves four.

RIVERVIEW CHARLIE'S

101 Flagler Avenue (904) 428-1865 Major Credit Cards
Lunch $7 Dinner $15

With a selection of up to a dozen freshly caught fish, from rainbow trout to golden tile, red snapper, yellowfin tuna, cobia or Mahi, this beautiful waterfront restaurant is as close to seafood paradise as it gets. Add choices of Maine African or Bahamian lobster, shrimp, scallops, oysters and crabs, all expertly prepared and you understand why Riverview Charlie's is a favorite port of call for boaters and land travelers alike. It could qualify as a meat lovers heaven as well with ribs, chops and black Angus beef, aged and chef cut on premises and cooked with perfection.

Its three tiers of dining provide fantastic views of sunsets over the waters where yachtsmen and dolphin play, but the "piece de resistance" is a Sunday Brunch one must experience to believe. Five chef stations offer every delicacy from omelettes and Belgian waffles to caviar and champagne. One table is filled with steamed shellfish while duck, chicken, fish, beef and vegetables are grilled outdoors. Owner Marsel Psomas insists the only items frozen at his Riverview Charlie's are homemade ice creams and sorbets. Cheers to this fine restaurateur!

Grilled Bahamian Lobster Feast

1 large Bahamian lobster
chefs seafood seasoning
3/4 cup dry white wine
1 lb sea scallops
2 med zucchini
2 med yellow squash
chopped dill mix

Steam whole lobster until shell is red and half done. Split lobster in half & clean out cavity. Place lobster shell side down in large skillet. Arrange scallops around, sprinkle with seafood seasoning & add white wine. Cover skillet & cook over medium high heat for 8 minutes. Turn scallops when half done. Meanwhile, slice zucchini & yellow squash, brush with oil & grill till done. Arrange lobster on platter, top with scallops & surround with grilled vegetables. Garnish with dill mix. Serves two.

THE COURTYARD ON GROVE

275 Tangerine Ave & Grove (407) 459-9736 Major Credit Cards
Lunch $6 Dinner $11 Sunday Brunch $6

What began as a small luncheon cafe, with eight seats and a few gift items, by Jerre Vogt and her daughter Daune, has grown in a short time to one of Merritt Island's most popular restaurants with seating for 130 guests and rooms filled with a wide array of artistic gifts. Originally geared towards healthy luncheons of homemade soups, sandwiches and quiche, they expanded their menus to include full course dinners with dishes from Teriyaki Scallops and Prime Rib, to Rack of Lamb or Chicken Janice. Fresh Mahi-Mahi, grouper or salmon are baked or broiled, topped with crab meat, asparagus or artichokes and Bernaise, Sherry or lemon dill sauces. Using fresh products and simple recipes with nothing fried, they serve a delicious selection of crepes, salads, pasta, breads and desserts all made from scratch. Jerre, with husband Jack, restored a 1926 vintage residence to its original beauty to create a homelike ambiance for romantic dining inside or in their tropical garden for lunch, starlite dinners or sunny Sunday brunch. For exceptional cuisine, atmosphere, gifts and hosts, visit The Courtyard on Grove!

Teriyaki Scallops

16 sea scallops, 30/40 count
8 bacon strips
6 tblsps teriyaki sauce
2 tblsps pineapple juice
pinch of granulated garlic
dash ground ginger

Wrap each scallop tightly with half a bacon strip and secure with a toothpick. Place in a baking pan and pour mixture of Teriyaki, pineapple juice, garlic and ginger over scallops. Bake in 350 degree oven for 10 to 12 minutes until scallops are just done and bacon is medium. Arrange scallops on dishes and pour hot sauce over. Garnish dish with fresh fruit and tomato rose.
Serves two as an appetizer.

MARINA GRILL

Melbourne Harbor 2210 S. Front St. (407) 724-6070 Major Credit Cards
Lunch $8 Dinner $15 Closed Sun & Mon Dinners

The setting overlooking yachts in the Melbourne Harbor Marina suggests that dining here is a rather casual affair either on their covered decks or inside in air conditioned comfort. It has, in fact, the perfect ambiance for cruising sailors and visitors looking for interesting places to enjoy a relaxed lunch or dinner. The cuisine, however, at Marina Grill is a far cry from typical waterfront fare and every item from a hobo salad of field greens with feta and oven roasted potatoes to a salmon in parchment entree could be considered a gourmet treat. The menu is printed daily listing new dishes like pita pizzas with chicken or shrimp, steak quesadilla or a teriyaki filet mignon with a red wine and portobello sauce. They are famous for huge summer salads topped with gorgonzola, feta, grilled sirloin, chicken or seafood. Even their California burger of grilled ground chuck with French goat cheese, sundried tomatoes and sauteed onions is sensational. Becky and Frank Billings have been creating these healthy culinary delights at their Marina Grill since 1992 and present a delicious change of taste for Melbourne Harbor.

Baked Chambord Brie in Puff Pastry

2 4 oz brie cheese wheels
6 oz chambord wild or mixed berry preserves
4 sheets puff pastry dough

Cut 2 sheets of pastry dough into 6" squares & spread top side evenly with chambord preserves. Gently coat brie wheels with preserves & place on pastry sheets. Wrap edges of dough over cheese & seal smoothly. Use remaining sheets of pastry to cut & shape flower arrangement on top of coated brie wheel. Bake in oven for 15 minutes at 350 degrees until golden brown. Spoon preserves on plates and top with baked brie. Garnish with apple slices & serve hot as an appetizer or as an after dinner dessert. Serves two.

CAPT. HIRAM'S

1606 N. Indian River Dr.   Marker 66 on ICW   (561) 589-4345
Lunch $6   Dinner $12   Major Credit Cards

Sailing south past Sebastian Inlet on the Intracoastal Waterway, you might think you had entered the Florida Keys, for just to starboard is a waterfront resort with a sand beach, palm trees and hotel typical of the islands. It is actually Capt. Hiram's, a restaurant built in 1986 by Tom Collins and Martin Carter in the style of Key West, complete with a "Sandbar", live music and the Captain's Quarters Motel, all with views of the waterfront and marina facilities. The menu includes chargrilled steaks, salads, chicken dishes and a variety of seafood including a fresh catch of the day, grilled, broiled, fried, Cajun or basted with Caribbean jerk spices as well as New England clam chowder, mussels, Maryland crab cakes and crab soup. Or, try oyster shooters, key lime pie, Bimini coffee and tropical drinks that make you feel you are dining in "the islands". Known as "The Happening Place on Sebastian riverfront", Capt. Hiram's also offers scenic river cruises, deep sea fishing, parasailing and jet skis as well as live entertainment for weekend parties. Here you will enjoy good food and great fun, all captured with the magic of The Keys!

Capt. Hiram's Shrimp Salad

2-1/2 lbs popcorn shrimp
2-1/2 lbs medium shrimp
1-1/4 lbs large shrimp
4 oz diced celery
4 oz diced green onions
3/4 tblsp celery seeds
3/4 tblsp black pepper
1 tblsp spicy Caribbean seasoning
1 tblsp Old Bay
1 qt Hellmann's mayonnaise

Cook, peel and drain shrimp. Add diced celery and green onions and stir in gently. Add celery seeds, black pepper, Caribbean and Old Bay seasonings and mix thoroughly. Add mayonnaise and fold gently to desired consistency. Serve as salad, appetizer or with platter of seafood. Serves 8 to 10.

OCEAN GRILL

Route 60 at the Ocean (561) 231-5409 Closed Sat. & Sun. Lunch
Lunch $8 Dinner $17 Major Credit Cards

Over 50 years ago, the Ocean Grill was built on sand dunes some 200 yards from the Atlantic. Today the ocean laps under this beautiful structure of pecky cypress and mahogany filled with wrought iron and Spanish antiques. The views both inside and out offer patrons a rare feeling of Florida in the early 40's while dining on fresh local grouper, pompano, red snapper and swordfish. Its reputation for the best seafood on the beach has been continued by the Replogle family for three decades, with its third generation now washing dishes and bussing tables.

As a family affair, everything is made in house from salad dressings to breads and desserts. Steaks are trimmed from loins of choice beef and freshly caught fish are hand cut, broiled, wood grilled or prepared cajun style to your liking. Chef Tim McGraw, a CIA grad, believes "simplicity is best" and his presentations of roast duckling, crab cakes or sesame crusted tuna are delicious proof of his culinary skills. The Ocean Grill combines years of experience with its family tradition of excellence to satisfy every guest with superb cuisine and great ocean views!

Sesame Crusted YellowfinTuna

4 9 oz tuna steaks
1 cup sesame seeds
1/4 lb butter, whipped
2 tblsps soy sauce
2 tsps sesame oil
1 tsp fresh chopped ginger
1/2 tsp fresh garlic
1 tblsp wasabi
1/4 cup chives, sliced thin

Coat tuna steaks with 1/2 cup of sesame seeds & sear on both sides in hot oil until seeds are golden. For sauce: Toast 1/2 cup of sesame seeds. Mix butter with soy sauce, ginger, garlic & wasabi. Add toasted sesame seeds & heat until pourable. Slice steaks on diagonal, arrange on plates and drizzle wasabi sauce over. Garnish with chives & lemon slices & serve with slaw. Serves four.

ELLIE'S

41 Royal Palm Blvd. (561) 778-2600 Major Cards
Dinner $18 Seasonal Closings

A graduate of La Varenne culinary school in Paris, Mark Gottwald spent years from New York to California developing his culinary style which he calls, "New American with classical French influences". Now, he and his wife Ellie divide their time between The Ships Inn on Nantucket and their second restaurant, Ellie's, located on the Intracoastal in Vero Beach. In season, gourmands enjoy the best of many worlds with New England scallops, fresh Florida seafood, steaks and lamb from Colorado or salmon from Canada. Ellie's ambiance, like Ships Inn, is understated elegance with gardens, lush greenery and fresh flowers creating a tropical atmosphere. Mark's culinary art is equally unpretentious, in his entrees of lamb with mint couscous and rosemary demi glace, duck breast with port bordelaise or steak au poivre with haricot vert. For more casual dining, the bar at Ellie's offers salads, seafood tempura, designer hamburgers or pastas, all with views of the waterways. Jackets and reservations are suggested, but the only requirement is that you be prepared for a truly sensational dining experience.

Duck Breast with Port Bordelaise

2 fresh duck breasts
2 tblsps vegetable oil
1 bottle Port
3 shallots, minced
2 sprigs thyme
2 sprigs parsley
1 bay leaf
6 black peppercorns
3 green peppercorns
1/4 cup demi-glace
1/4 lb unsalted butter
salt & pepper to taste

Diagonally score breasts on both sides & sear in hot oil, skin side first. Finish in 400 degree oven for 5 mins. Let rest & carve into diagonal slices. For sauce, combine Port with next 5 ingredients & reduce by 4/5. Strain, add green peppercorns, demi-glace & whisk in butter. Fan slices on plates, spoon sauce over & serve with sweet potato pancake & snow peas. Serves four.

CONCHY JOE'S SEAFOOD

3945 N.E. Indian River Drive (561) 334-1130 Major Credit Cards
Lunch $6 Dinner $13

If you've ever wondered what Florida life was like in the roaring 30's you only have to visit this old riverfront fishhouse called Conchy Joe's. The walls of this seafood restaurant and bar are lined with antique fish mounts and memorabilia that retrace the history of rum runners and fishboat captains who dined here for decades. Today, owner Fred Ayres has retained that prohibition era ambiance with daily happy hours that feature tropical drinks and a raw bar and lounge with every item from alligator tidbits to BBQ boar ribs. Conchy Joe's specializes in Native and Bahamian dishes of freshly caught local swordfish, grouper and dolphin, broiled, grilled or simmered with pineapple and rum, a la Grand Cay. The conch burgers, fritters and salads are unmatched and both Bon Appetit and Gourmet would love the secret to their conch chowder recipe. Conchy's also grills Certified Angus steaks over oak logs in a brick fireplace for non-seafood lovers. If you really want to kick back with a Hemingway Daiquiri and enjoy some delicious seafood and good old fashion Florida fun and hospitality with a waterfront view, this is the place!

Dolphin Grand Cay

2 fresh dolphin fillets
1 fresh pineapple
4 oz light rum
flour
egg wash
1 tblsp butter for cooking
2 tblsps sugar
1 cup Myers rum
1 lime
3 tblsps chilled butter
salt & pepper

Cut fillets into 4 servings & dredge in flour seasoned with salt & pepper. Coat in egg wash & ligltly brown both sides in butter. Do not cook through. Add light rum & reduce to a simmer. Add pineapple, cut into 1 inch chunks & 1/2 of dark rum. Sprinkle with sugar & stir gently. Season with salt & pepper, add butter & rest of dark rum. Squeeze lime over all & gently stir. Serve fillets with pineapple chunks & rum sauce. Serves four.

DOCKSIDE

131 S.W. Flagler Avenue (561) 219-3625 Major Cards
Dinner $12

With its warm wood columns and walls, cathedral ceilings, paintings, gold fixtures and etched glass panels it is perhaps the most visually pleasing dining room you will find anywhere. There is a large separate bar area with a grand piano, a gorgeous waiting lounge and practically every table offers a fantastic panorama of the St. Lucie River and the dramatic Roosevelt Bridge. Yet the most attractive jewel in this restaurant's crown is Lenh Dombrose, who is seldom seen except through her culinary artistry as chef and co-owner with husband Arthur.

Every presentation, from a Scampitizer or Crab Meat Prentis appetizers, to her pan seared Sesame Crusted Tuna or Rack of Lamb is as appealing to the eye as to the palate. Steaks, fresh fish daily, Chateaubriand and pastas have made Dockside a favorite for both residents and visitors to Stuart's quaint new waterfront. Two huge billfish mounted atop Dockside make it a perfect landmark for boaters cruising the Okeechobee and the ICW. But it is Lenh's Asian heritage and her 30 years as a chef that make dining here a truly delicious and rewarding experience.

Black Sesame Crusted Tuna with Grilled Shrimp

1 lb fresh tuna steak
black sesame seeds
vegetable oil
6 jumbo shrimp
2 plantains
sweet potato chips
1 cup mashed potatoes
red, yellow & green peppers & chives for garnish

Coat tuna thoroughly with black sesame seeds. Pan sear tuna in hot vegetable oil on all sides till just rare. Meanwhile peel & devein shrimp leaving tails on. Grill shrimp on both sides until just done & pink. Deep fry plantains & sweet potato chips until crisp. Stand shrimp on scoop of mashed potatoes & arrange tuna slices around. Garnish with fried plantains, sweet potato chips, sliced chives & peppers. Serves two.

Stuart

FLAGLER GRILL

47 S.W. Flagler Avenue (561) 221-9517 Seasonal Hours
Dinner $19 AE VISA MC

There is a casual elegance about this restaurant reminiscent of dining in Soho or Little Italy, except that owners Linda and Paul Daly exude a warm and friendly ambiance seldom found in N.Y. Their American and Floridian cuisine, prepared in an open kitchen, with no microwave, warming plates or canned goods, offers fresh local seafood, Midwestern beef and at least three special entrees nightly. Chef George Dahlstrom may feature elk or venison with a butternut squash puree, a peppered leg of lamb with polenta and ratatouille or perhaps a Chilean sea bass sauteed Thai style with two curries over coucous. All breads and desserts like his layered cheesecake with mango, raspberry and kiwi are prepared in house as well as his homemade ravioli. The entire restaurant is now non-smoking including their new martini bar with a dozen choices from gin classics to vodka with Godiva. To compliment their creative cuisine the cellar houses some 130 American and foreign wines. With its decor and decorum, culinary artistry and homelike hospitality it is little wonder why the Flagler Grill is the favorite in Stuart.

Venison Chops w/ Demi Glace

8 bone venison rack
1/2 cup olive oil
zest of 1 orange
3 sprigs rosemary
2 tblsps cracked pepper
2 tblsps chopped garlic

Cut venison into 8 frenched chops & marinate in next 5 ingredients, covered & refrigerated for 4 hours. For demi glace, place 2 carrots & 2 onions, rough cut into 1-1/2 cups red wine with 8 peppercorns, 2 bay leaves & 4 garlic cloves. Reduce till dry, add 4 cups veal stock & reduce by 2/3. Season chops with salt & pepper & grill to desired temperature. Stand chops over scoop of garlic mashed potatoes & ladle butternut squash puree & demiglace around. Garnish with red pearl onions & sauteed spinach. Serves four.

Southern Florida mm 984 to 1095

The southern third of the state has been the playground of America ever since "the boom days" of the 1920's when Henry Flagler built his railroad from Chicago to Miami. Tourists by the thousands arrived to enjoy a vacation in the sun and escape the cold of the North. Today over 7 million people reside here and the population still expands during the winter season when the "snowbirds" flock to these warm southern shores. Besides its beautiful beaches and fabulous resort hotels, there is no end of things to see and do. There are dog and thoroughbred races or Jai Alai, off-shore fishing, golf and tennis, shopping and visiting museums, tropical gardens or cruising along the Intracoastal Waterway. But dining out on haute cuisine in elegant surroundings or just enjoying fresh seafood in a casual waterfront cafe at any of the following restaurants has to be the ultimate pastime for every visitor here!

THE CRAB HOUSE

1065 N. Hwy Alt. A1A Jupiter Inlet (561) 744-1300 Major Credit Cards
Lunch $6 Dinner $11

One approaches The Crab House down a beautiful pathway lined with tropical plants and flowers, or you can arrive by boat on the Loxahatchee River beside the famous Jupiter lighthouse. From any direction this is a great place to relax, roll up your sleeves, dig into some delicious fresh seafood and enjoy a parade of yachts sailing by on the Intracoastal Waterway. The first Crab House opened in Miami back in 1976 and was so popular they've grown to six locations along the ICW including Aventura, Lauderhill, Boca Raton and Plantation. At any one you'll find a delicious variety of crustaceans, from true Chesapeake Bay style blue crabs and soft shells or Alaskan king and snow crabs to Florida's famous stone crab claws. Add to this a dozen choices of fresh fish including Atlantic salmon, tilapia and wahoo, cooked to your liking. Clams casino, oysters Rockefeller, gater bites or popcorn shrimp and Cajun crawfish tails along with steaks and pastas make The Crab House a fun place to dine for kids and adults. For serious lovers of seafood and a unique setting for private parties and group functions, this is it!

Stuffed Lobster & Alaskan Snow Crab

1 whole Maine lobster
2 8 oz snow crab clusters
8 oz Crab Imperial
1 tblsp paprika
1 tblsp Morton's natural seasoning
2 oz lemon butter
1 lb cooked potatoes
2 tblsps chopped parsley

Steam whole lobster until half cooked. Remove, split in half & clean cavity. Stuff cavities with Crab Imperial mixture and brush all with lemon butter. Cook in 500 degree convection oven for 5 to 7 minutes. Sprinkle seasonings and cook for 1 minute. Place on platter and serve with steamed snow crab cluster, parsley potatoes and melted butter. Garnish plate with lemon wedge and kale.
Serves two.

CAPT. CHARLIE'S REEF GRILL

12846 U.S. Highway 1 (561) 624-9924 VISA MC
Lunch $6 Dinner $10

It is practically hidden on the side of a mini-mall with no signage visible from Route 1, they have never spent a dime on advertising and reservations are next to impossible. But still, locals and visitors lucky enough to find them and a few celebrities will line up every day for their doors to open at five. There is nothing fancy about the decor and the three dining areas are small, but the food that comes out of an open kitchen is the indescribably best you will find in Juno Beach. It may be called Florida regional with Spanish or island influences, but their nightly menu lists nearly 40 Tapas, a dozen fresh fish specials and creative entrees like rock shrimp and gorgonzola fettucini, Cuban crabcakes or Key West chicken. Yellow tail snapper Bahamian style, peppered tuna with a blueberry teriyaki sauce or grilled quail all come in large portions at small cost as do their wines at bargain prices. By popular demand owners Mary Beth and Ross Matheson opened a second place, literally and figuratively "Three Door Up" for lunches and waiting lounge for Reef Grill patrons. For superb cuisine, service and personalities, find this place!

Bahamian Snapper with Tropical Slaw

4 whole yellow tail snapper
1/2 cup orange juice
3 garlic cloves, minced
1 chili pepper, minced
kosher salt
canola oil
4 plantains
2 cups tropical slaw

Clean fish leaving head & tail on. Score on both sides & marinate in orange juice, garlic & peppers for 1 hour. Sprinkle with salt & deep fry in hot oil until just done & crisp. For slaw: Combine 1/2 cup each chopped pineapple, pear, apple, tomato, cucumber, scallions & red pepper with 4 tblsps fennel, 2 tblsps honey & juice of 1 orange & lime. Season with salt & fresh black pepper. Pour a little marinade over fish and serve with slaw and fried plantains. Serves two.

WATERWAY CAFE

2300 PGA Boulevard (561) 694-1700 AE VISA MC
Lunch $7 Dinner $12

Sitting right on the waterway, this casual open air restaurant has been a favorite of both locals and visitors in North Palm Beach for over 13 years. With a nautical decor of huge carved wooden fish, three antique Ivy League rowing skulls and the only floating bar in Florida, it is the ideal port of call for boaters on the ICW cruising for good food and fun. Their menu would appeal to any age or taste, listing items from Florida stone crab claws to Italiano, Mexican or spicy Thai pizzas, cooked in a wood fired oven. Chef Bill Hessenauer is masterful with freshly caught dolphin, salmon and tuna he serves blackened, grilled or teriyaki style. His conch fritters with a key lime mustard sauce, smoked chicken penne or the Waterway linguine filled with crab, shrimp and scallops and a spinach tomato sauce are outstanding presentations, as are all his nightly specials. The service is courteous and prompt, portions generous, and prices quite modest. Live entertainment packs both bars with local revelers who come by boat and car to dine, drink and dance the night away at the Waterway Cafe, a happening place!

Waterway Seafood Linguini w/ Tomato Basil Sauce

8 oz fresh sea scallops
8 oz med shrimp, cleaned
2 tblsps olive oil
8 oz fresh spinach leaves
8 oz lump crab meat
1 lb linguine

Saute scallops & shrimp in hot olive oil 3 to 4 minutes. Meanwhile, to make sauce: Saute 1 tblsp each of fresh chopped garlic & shallots in 6 oz butter till brown. Add 1 can diced tomatoes, 1 tblsp salt, 1 tblsp black pepper, 1 tblsp fresh chopped basil & 1/2 pint heavy cream & simmer 20 minutes. Add spinach & tomato basil sauce to shrimp mixture & simmer 3 to 4 minutes. Cook linguine al dente & divide onto 4 plates. Spoon sauce over & top with crab meat. Garnish with parsley & scallions. Serves four.

SPOTO'S OYSTER BAR

125 Datura Street (561) 835-1828 Major Credit Cards
Lunch $6 Dinner $8

There are oyster bars and then there is Spoto's Oyster Bar. With mirrored walls and mahogany bars, booths with lovely shell patterned fabrics, art deco ceilings and the freshest selection of shellfish in West Palm, this is as close to mollusk heaven as it gets. With 17 years in the seafood industry, owner John Spoto and chef Bill Flatley, who grew up on his father's oyster boat, combined talents to create a seafood restaurant "par excellence". In addition to freshly shucked Blue Point, Wellfleet or Malpeque oysters, Spoto's also features clams, mussels, lobster and crabmeat in unique chowders and stews, appetizers, salads, sandwiches and pastas. In an open kitchen, they prepare tuna sushimi, New Orleans crab cakes, Thai shrimp, Pacific rim grouper or Nantucket scallops from a menu of incredible seafood combinations. Oysters raw, pan fried, Rockefeller, baked with brie, as a shooter and steamed in a stew are just part of Spoto's philosophy of serving "good for the soul food" in a fun filled atmosphere. Only a block off Lake Worth in downtown West Palm Beach, Spoto's Oyster Bar rates two thumbs up!

Baked Brie Oysters with Champagne Sauce

16 fresh oysters in shells
1 lb brie cheese
4 tblsps finely chopped dill
4 oz butter, room temp
4 tblsps flour
1 qt heavy cream
2 cups champagne

Open shells leaving oyster in larger bottom shell. Place four to a plate on rock salt. Meanwhile, combine champagne and heavy cream and simmer for 4 minutes. Mix flour and butter, add to cream mixture and stir over low heat until thickened. Add dill and let cool. Pour 2 teaspoons of sauce over each oyster and top with a 1 ounce slice of brie. Bake 2 to 3 minutes in 350 oven and finish in broiler until brie is crunchy brown. Garnish with fresh parsley. Serves four.

TESTA'S

221 Royal Poinciana Way (561) 832-0992 Major Cards
Brkfst $4 Lunch $7 Dinner $12

It was opened in 1921 by Michael Testa, Sr. during the era of the Vanderbilts and Flaglers and after four generations of family pride and tradition it is still considered "The Grande Dame" of restaurants in Palm Beach. While menus and cuisine may have changed over the years, the freshness of their open air garden and the warm mahogany booths have still retained the ambiance of a time "gone by". Approaching an 80th anniversary, their breakfasts, lunches and dinners are as creative as ever, offering dishes from Testa's famous grilled tuna steak and classic crabcakes to Florida stone crab claws and seafood marinara. Their "Steak for Two", carved tableside, won the "Beef Backer" award and for seafood lovers their catch of the day is unrivaled for freshness and preparation. Long time patrons still enjoy Testa's homemade soups, salads, pastas and desserts, like their old fashion cakes and strawberry pie. They now stay open all year with a new tropical courtyard for outdoor dining, but with every change, Testa's maintains a standard of excellence and impeccable service set by the family decades ago.

Testa's Cream of Crab Soup

1-1/2 lbs lump crabmeat
1/4 cup crab base
1-1/4 cups chopped onions
2 qts heavy cream
2 qts half & half
1-1/4 lbs butter
5 drops tabasco
1-1/2 cups flour
1/2 tsp salt
2 celery stalks, minced
1/2 tsp white pepper
1-1/2 tsps Worchestershire
1-1/2 tsps Old Bay seasoning

Saute onions & celery in butter until tender. Add flour to make roux. Slowly add cream & whisk until there are no lumps. Add remaining ingredients & cook over medium heat until desired thickness. Yields approximately 2 gallons of soup.

CHUCK & HAROLD'S

207 Royal Poinciana Way (561) 659-1440 Major Credit Cards
Brkfst $5 Lunch $8 Dinner $15

It may appear that almost everything you find at Chuck & Harold's is offered in a large size, starting from an outside patio with open-air views of Royal Poinciana Way. Then there is a huge roof over an inside courtyard that retracts for dining and dancing under the stars. They present six different menus, oversized of course to include hundreds of choices available throughout the day, from a breakfast of lox and bagels or a lobster and shrimp omelette, to Gourmet Munchies like soft shell crabs or carpaccio at midnight. At lunch a Big Fish Killer Club means what it says and a dozen super size salads fill large bowls and appetites. Brunch on Sunday is a bountiful banquet of Bloody Marys, Belgium waffles or Boston scrod and Harold burgers. Special Twilight Dinners serve four courses with the only thing small at Chuck & Harold's, the check. Their dinner entrees feature creative dishes like Cognac lobster Provencale, B.B.Q. baby back ribs, crabmeat and asparagus crusted dolphin and 10 dishes called "Shrimply Paradise". Since 1981 Chuck & Harold's has been a " large" part of the culinary life of Palm Beach.

Asparagus Crusted Dolphin

2 8 oz dolphin fillets
10 asparagus sprigs
4 oz lump crabmeat
2 oz croutons
1 cup tropical salsa
1 cup cooked couscous

Blanch asparagus, cut into small pieces & mix well with lump crabmeat & croutons. Coat dolphin with asparagus mixture & bake in 350 degrees oven for 8 minutes or until golden brown. Meanwhile, to make salsa, combine 2 oz each of sliced mango, papaya & watermelon with 2 oz each of chopped green onions & cilantro. Add 2 tblsps lemon juice & sprinkle with sugar. Mound couscous on plates, top with dolphin fillets & spoon salsa around. Garnish with red & green pepper strips. Serves two.

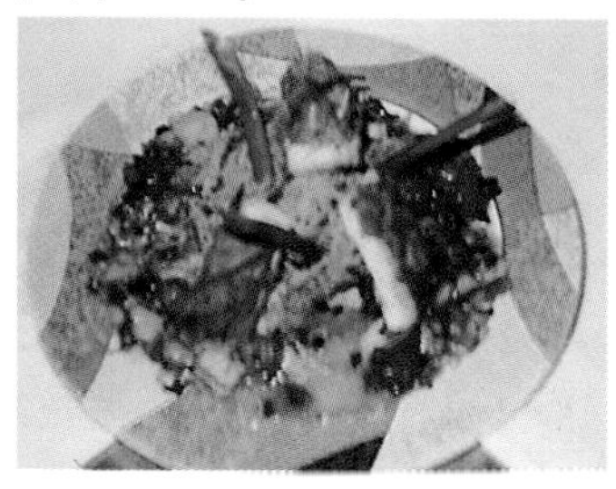

THE BUCCANEER

Buccaneer Marina 142 Lake Dr. (561) 844-3477 Major Credit Cards
Lunch $7 Dinner $16

Whenever you find a restaurant like The Buccaneer with a fleet of sportsfishing boats docked outside and their captains lining the bar, you can bet the menu and cuisine is going to be exceptional. Fish trophies, photographs, etched glass ships beside beautiful wood paneled walls add to a nautical ambiance with wide views of the waterways just outside. It is the ideal setting to enjoy the creations of a dedicated kitchen whose presentations of veal, beef, lamb, poultry, and seafood are outstanding. Their sauteed grouper with shrimp and Andouille sausage, sesame encrusted tuna or the chargrilled salmon with a shiitake cream sauce would satisfy any lover of seafood. If you prefer, the bourbon marinated pork loin, rack of lamb, Chateaubriand or veal gruyere are equally delicious. Shellfish are flown from North Atlantic waters and everything from lobster bisque to breads and salad dressings are made on premises. The Lounge is famous for their happy hours with hors d'oeuvres and "do-it-yourself" weekend Bloodies. The Buccaneer can take great pride for 40 years of individual attention and dedication to their patrons.

Sauteed Grouper w/ Shrimp, Sausage & Red Pepper Coulis

4 8 oz grouper fillets
olive oil
flour
salt & pepper
20 rock shrimp
4 oz Andouille sausage
1 cup red pepper coulis
1 cup beurre blanc

Salt & pepper grouper fillets, dredge in flour & saute in olive oil until just done. Meanwhile peel rock shrimp & saute in olive oil with diced sausage until just done. Add red pepper coulis & keep warm. Blend in beurre blanc just before serving. Arrange fillets on plate, spoon shrimp & sausage coulis on side & serve with spaghetti squash, steamed asparagus & wild rice. Serves four.

Fort Lauderdale *mm 1060*

With a metropolitan area laced with some 250 miles of beautiful canals and waterways, Fort Lauderdale can justly be called "The Venice of America". And this aquatic mecca for boaters also makes it what many consider to be "The Yachting Capitol of the World". Both are fairly accurate descriptions of this unique tropical paradise where soft sand beaches, swaying palms and shimmering blue waters provide the perfect setting for sunning, swimming, sailing and sightseeing. The area boasts some 50 golf courses, 500 tennis courts, soccer and baseball, museums, parks and a treasure of family activities as well as nightspots for sizzling entertainment and dancing. For cruising boaters, the Intracoastal is lined with marinas and the Las Olas River and Boulevard offer docking within blocks of chic shops and outstanding restaurants. Here is a selection of the city's very best.

YESTERDAY'S

3001 E. Oakland Park Blvd.   (954) 561-4400   Major Cards
Dinner $19

The Red Snapper Pontchartrain with Alaskan crab, shrimp, bearnaise sauce and toasted almonds is typical of the classic culinary presentations of executive chefs John Hisgen and Jean Claude Mille at this elegant waterfront restaurant in Fort Lauderdale. Their menus change with seasons and the availability of fresh seafood and ingredients, but every item from a Sesame Seared Sashimi first course to lobster, prime rib, catch of the day, shrimp scampi, Beef Wellington or Key West Chicken make Yesterday's a delectable dining experience. They are awarded not only for excellent cuisine, but for their gorgeous interior with three levels of seating that provide every guest with breathtaking views of the Intracoastal Waterway just outside. For company dinners, private cocktail parties, even weddings and receptions, their outstanding chefs and attentive staff will cater to your every need from elaborate banquets and lavish buffets to an intimate dinner for two. For a most memorable evening featuring delicious cuisine with romantic ambiance and superb service, Yesterday's is one of the very, very best.

Red Snapper Pontchartrain

2 8 oz red snapper fillets
4 large shrimp
2 oz crabmeat
1/4 cup white wine
5 tblsps flour
1 tsp minced shallots
1 cup bernaise sauce
1 cup cooked rice

Lightly coat snapper in flour, season with salt & pepper & saute in medium hot oil for 1-1/2 minutes on each side. Remove snapper & deglaze pan with wine. Stir for 2 minutes & add crabmeat, shrimp & garlic. Saute 1-1/2 minutes. Place snapper over bed of rice & top with crabmeat & shrimp mixture. Lace bearnaise sauce on top & place under broiler until light brown. Top with toasted almonds & serve with vegetables. Garnish with crisp plantains & cilantro. Serves two.

THE FRENCH QUARTER

Las Olas 215 SE 8th Avenue (954) 463-8000 Major Credit Cards
Lunch $9 Dinner $19 Closed Sunday

Swiss born Louis Flematti started in the 60's as a waiter in a small bistro on Las Olas Boulevard. Today, he owns Le Cafe de Paris in that same location as well as The French Quarter, an elegant restaurant with the ambiance of Old New Orleans just one block away. Here one dines in a secluded, intimate and timeless atmosphere of brick archways, skylit ceilings, gas lights, antiques, tuxedoed waiters and strolling musicians. In this romantic setting, you enjoy impeccable French cuisine, Creole and Continental specialties like roast Duck A L'Orange, Frog Legs Bayou, Beef Wellington and Rack of Lamb Bouquetierre. Epicurean delights from Pate du Chef Jean-Marie to Baked Alaska are as authentic and delicious as you would find anywhere in France. The delights of Chef Andreas, Veal Cordon Bleu, Dover Sole or Coquille St. Jacques at Le Cafe de Paris remind one of casual dining in a Parisian sidewalk cafe. With an extensive wine cellar, private party rooms, a bar for jazz and dancing, superb service and classic French cuisine, Louis provides a culinary trip to Paris from the heart of Las Olas!

Chicken Crepes Primavera

12 crepes
3 cups cooked chicken
8 oz diced mushrooms
2 tblsps butter
3/4 cups each shredded Provolone, Parmesan & Swiss cheese
1/4 tsp paprika
3 cups broccoli flowerets
3 cups white sauce
1/2 cup dry sherry

For filling: saute mushrooms in butter till limp. Let cool, add cubed chicken & 1 cup of basic white sauce laced with sherry. Brown one side of each crepe & spread with filling. Top with broccoli flowerets & roll up. Place crepes seam side down in greased gratin dish & cover with remaining white sauce. Sprinkle with mix of three cheeses & bake in 375° oven for 10 to 12 minutes. Serve with vegetables & rice. Serves six.

THE LEFT BANK

214 Southeast 6th Avenue (954) 462-5376 Major Cards
Dinner $22

In Paris this restaurant would be known as "Rive Gauche" and would probably be considered among the best that line the banks of the Seine. But unlike most French fare with butter and creams, this Left Bank in Fort Lauderdale features the cuisines of Provence, relying on fresh vegetables, herbs, garlic and olive oil to compliment the natural flavors of fish, game and poultry. Chef Jean-Pierre Brehier has evolved to these deliciously healthy dishes as a television host, in his cooking school, cookbook series and for his Left Bank patrons over 22 years.

Brehier's passion for cooking is evident in an ever changing menu and in every presentation from a Salmon and Shrimp Strudel appetizer to a crispy Long Island Duckling or a Dijon and Corn Crusted Lamb Loin dinner entree. His inherited French-Italian cooking talents, combined with fresh tropical and local ingredients and his charisma in the kitchen, assure Left Bank guests an evening of Incredible Cuisine with Chef Jean-Pierre Brehier (his new book title as well). Little wonder why Conde Nast voted it as one of the best 100 restaurants in America !

Dijon & Sweet Corn Crusted Lamb Loin

2 8 bone lamb loins
2 tblsps extra virgin olive oil
1/4 cup sweet corn kernels dried & chopped
1/4 cup dijon mustard
1/2 cup corn meal
2 tsps herb de provence

Combine corn, dijon, corn meal & herbs to make a paste. Pan sear lamb loins in hot olive oil. Let cool & coat loins with paste. Cook in 350° oven for 15 minutes for medium. For sauce: Sweat 2 tblsps chopped sage with 1 tsp chopped fresh sage & 6 oz of wild mushrooms for 2 minutes. Add 1 cup cabernet sauvignon & reduce by half. Add 2 cups beef stock & reduce by half. Slice loins & arrange over baby vegetables. Spoon sauce around & garnish with fresh rosemary. Serves two.

PUSSER'S® at the Beach

429 South Atlantic Blvd. (954) 527-2544 Major Credit Cards
Lunch $7 Dinner $13

Every Pusser's location from the Virgin Islands to Annapolis offers guests superb cuisine, service, decor and panoramic waterfront views. Pusser's at the Beach in Ft. Lauderdale is no exception where diners sit under palms beside a waterfall overlooking a blue Atlantic and miles of pure white sand beach. Steel bands, reggae music and a brightly clad wait staff add to the ambiance typical of life in the islands. The menu focuses on seafood and Caribbean fare like stone crab claws and crab cakes and West Indian specialties. Tortola black bean soup, conch fritters, Jamaican chicken in a spicy BBQ sauce or coconut fried fish are tried and tested favorites from the BVI's. Another special dish is an Asian vegetable stir fry with chicken, shrimp or scallops that's exceptional! Of course no visit is complete without a legendary Pusser's Painkiller, first concocted on the island of Jost Van Dyke. Aside from great food and drink and fantastic views, their adjoining Co. Store offers a great selection of Pusser's exclusive line of tropical and nautical clothing and unique accessories. This place really has it all!

Shrimp, Scallops & Vegetable Stir Fry

24 medium shrimp
24 Bay scallops
2 lbs mixed vegetables: baby corn, snow peas, shredded green cabbage, sliced carrots, chopped celery & bokchoy, red & green peppers julienned, sliced mushrooms & broccoli flowrettes
4 tblsps stir fry sauce
4 tblsps chopped garlic
16 oz cooked rice

Heat 4 oz oil in large saute pan. Add vegetables, garlic & cook for 1 minute. Add shrimp, scallops & stir fry sauce & cook 2 minutes or until just done & al dente. Place rice in center of plates, spoon vegetable mix around rice with shrimp & scallops arranged on top. Serves four.

CALIFORNIA CAFE

2301 SE 17th Street Causeway at Pier 66 (954) 728-3500
Lunch $9 Dinner $17 Major Cards

After some five years at famed Pier 66, the California Cafe Bar & Grill is still blowing a breath of fresh air across the culinary waters of Ft. Lauderdale. From its panoramic perch overlooking luxury yachts in the adjacent marina and Intracoastal Waterway to its modern artistic decor and dramatic lighting, this West Coast transplant has created a setting as spectacular and unique as its eclectic cuisine. Their menu is not only Californian, but a blending of Pacific Rim style and flavors with Caribbean, Mediterranean and local influences offering light and tasty foods from Hawaiian Tuna Sashimi to gourmet pizzas and Rosemary Chicken roasted in a wood burning oven. The abundance of fresh Florida seafood is seasonally featured like plantain crusted dolphin, pepper grilled tuna and crab crusted sea bass. Smoked rack of pork, spicy baby back ribs or braised Colorado lamb shanks will satisfy any meat lover as do their salads and pastas for lighter lunches. Dining at California Cafe Bar & Grill is like a delicious and delightful culinary vacation to a tropical island or the far West Coast...all without leaving Pier 66!

Hawaiian Style Tuna Sashimi

12 oz sushi grade tuna
2 tblsps macadamia nuts, toasted & chopped
1 tblsp Hijiki
1 green onion, sliced thin
2 tsps minced garlic
2 oz sesame oil
1 oz tamari
pineapple salsa
cucumber salsa
pickled ginger
2 coconuts
ginger sauce
cilantro wasabi oil

Dice tuna into small cubes, toss with next 6 ingredients & chill. To arrange, place two salsas & pickled ginger on plate corners. Drizzle ginger sauce & wasabi oil on plates. Place tuna mix in coconut halves & garnish with fried plantain slices, julienned carrots & bean sprouts.
Serves four as appetizers.

LA MARINA

Marriott Marina 1881 S.E. 17th Street (954) 463-4000 Major Cards
Lunch $7 Dinner $17

The Marriott Marina in Ft. Lauderdale is one of those rare places where boaters may tie up alongside and enjoy a superb dinner as well as the comfort of an elegant room ashore. Both hotel and restaurant provide guests and patrons with panoramic views of the busy Intracoatal Waterway within easy access to the Atlantic Ocean. It is an ideal port of call to enjoy the sights of this world famous yachting capitol along with culinary treats from La Marina, a waterfront restaurant offering a superb selection of cuisine for breakfast, lunch and dinner. For starters, try their award winning Shrimp Robusto with black bean salsa or a Jerk Chicken Breast appetizer with avocado and pineapple mojo. Fresh tropical flavored seafood like Sofrito Shrimp, Creole Dolphin or banana crusted Yellow Tail Snapper are entree favorites as is the Captain's cut roast prime rib and a special bread pudding dessert with rum sauce. Be sure to save room and stay for a Sunday Brunch that fills La Marina with tables of mid-day delights to satisfy any taste. By land or sea it's a great dining place to be.

Sofrito Marinated Grilled Shrimp

12 jumbo shrimp
1 large green pepper
2 large garlic cloves
10 cilantro leaves
15 parsley leaves
2 oz olive oil
1 cup tri-tomato relish
10 oz cooked yellow rice with black beans, red & green peppers

For sofrito marinade: Saute chopped green pepper & garlic in olive oil until transparent. Remove & add chopped cilantro & parsley. Let cool & blend to a puree. Split shrimp leaving shells on & clean. Coat shrimp in marinade & charcoal grill until cooked but tender. Spoon rice down center of plates & top with pairs of overlapping shrimp. Border rice with tomato relish & garnish with large cilantro leaves. Serves two.

15th STREET FISHERIES

1900 S.E.15th Street (954) 763-2777 Major Credit Cards
Lunch $8 Dinner $18

After twenty years on the waterfront both the 15th Street Fisheries and its owner, Michael Hurst are considered treasures in Fort Lauderdale. The restaurant for its consistently fresh seafood, choice meats and museum like decor with the friendliest service around, and Michael for his zany sense of humor and sincere hospitality for every guest who dines here. There are two floors for dining filled with authentic artifacts with the ambiance of a turn-of-the-century seafood processing plant. Each room provides guests with views of the busy ICW and a daily pelican feeding show Hurst began years ago. He once brought a baby elephant to happy hour, but when it comes to his patrons he is very serious about serving his salads ice cold, and food piping hot. He buys snapper, grouper, tuna and other Florida fish whole to ensure freshness and prepares only the choicest cuts of meat. Lobsters from Maine, New Zealand or local waters are on the menu as well as their High Adventure items of alligator, ostrich and flying fish. For a tasty, friendly and fun filled meal to remember, Michael Hurst and his 15th Street Fisheries are a must.

Flounder with Crabmeat Stuffing

4 4 oz fillets of flounder
1 cup lump crabmeat
1 celery stalk
1 tblsp mustard seed
1/2 cup white wine
1/2 cup buerre blanc sauce
chopped parsley
salt & pepper

Finely chop celery stalk, combine with mustard seed & gently mix with lump crabmeat. Divide & place mixture between two pieces of flounder fillets. Place stuffed flounder fillets on baking dishes & season with salt and pepper. Add 1/4 cup white wine to each dish & bake in 350 degree oven for 10 minutes or until flounder is browned. Top each dish with buerre blanc & garnish with chopped parsley. Serve with home fried potato chips and cole slaw. Serves two.

CHEF'S PALETTE

1650 S.E. 17th Street (954) 760-7957 Closed Sat. & Sun. Lunch
Lunch $7 Dinner $14

This may be the only restaurant you will find surrounded by glassed-in kitchens with literally dozens of chefs preparing succulent dishes for your lunch and dinner. They are in fact students in residency at The School of Culinary Arts in Ft. Lauderdale, studying towards careers as professional chefs under the watchful eyes of skilled instructors and Master Chef Klaus Friedenreich. As Director of Culinary Arts, he contributes a wealth of international experience that is evident in every course offered, from classic French, Italian and Chinese to American Regional cooking. Patrons at this unique restaurant are rewarded with delicious culinary artistry, styled and served to perfection at half the expected cost. Island pork chops with corn and pepper salsa, pan seared duck breast or potato crusted salmon are typical of the talents of these aspiring young chefs. Twice monthly, guests are treated to demonstrations of their evening meal with recipes and instruction by Chef Klaus. For novice or aspiring cooks and inquisitive gourmets, The Chef's Palette is a colorful introduction to fine dining art!

Potato Crusted Salmon

2 4 oz salmon fillets
4 potatoes
flour for dusting
oil for sauteing
2 zucchini
2 carrots
2 oz butter
4 oz tomato basil sauce

Spiral cut and julienne the potatoes. Dust the salmon fillets with flour and coat with julienned potatoes. Place wrapped salmon in a hot pan with a little oil and saute until golden brown. Turn and saute other side until golden. Meanwhile, julienne the zucchini and carrots and saute in butter until tender crisp. Place bed of vegetables on plates and top with salmon fillets. Spoon tomato basil sauce around. Serves two.

BIMINI BOATYARD

1555 S.E. 17th Street (954) 525-7400 Major Credit Cards
Lunch $8 Dinner $11

This is considered the best restaurant in Ft. Lauderdale where you arrive by car or boat, let your hair down and enjoy an exceptional selection of varied cuisine in an upscale atmosphere. Bimini certainly denotes an island ambiance, but boatyard hardly describes a beautifully detailed interior with open views of outdoor patios and luxury yachts tied alongside. The daily happy hours are ideal for meeting or making friends among boaters, residents and visitors, and it is said to be the "best place to snag a millionaire". It seems everything at Bimini Boatyard Bar & Grill is designed to make their guests feel both classy and comfortable, from the decor and service to a menu that offers an eclectic selection of fresh seafood to a wild assortment of steaks, lamb, veal and chicken entrees. There's a new Italian menu for pasta lovers and the Bimini Sunday Brunch is an incredible way to jump start any week. Their lunch menu lists dozens of sandwiches and salads from classic Cobb to warm lobster. Bimini Boatyard continues as the "in" place to enjoy great food and fantastic happy hours with great friends....old and new!

Spaghettini Al Frutti Di Mare

12 medium shrimp
8 oz fresh scallops
12 oz fresh grouper
3 cups spaghetti sauce
dash of red pepper
1/2 cup white wine
butter
2 lbs spaghettini, cooked al dente
Parmesan cheese
fresh basil

Peel and devein shrimp and cut grouper into bite size pieces. Season seafood lightly with salt & pepper and saute in butter briefly until half done. Add white wine and crushed red pepper and simmer. Add spaghetti sauce and heat through. Place spaghettini into bowls, spoon seafood mixture over and sprinkle with parmesan cheese and chopped basil. Serves four.

Miami *mm 1077*

It is hard to imagine when looking at Miami's skyline that less than a century ago it was just a small town on the edge of the Everglades. Today its huge towers of steel and glass are home to some 4,000 companies and more than 150 banks that make it an international center for finance and trade for the Caribbean and South America. But looking beyond the skyscrapers one discovers a city of contrasts, with colorful Cuban and Haitian communities and the world's leading cruise port, to palm trees and balmy sea breezes of her sister city, Miami Beach. Over 400 hotels, from old Art Deco landmarks to fabulous seaside resorts, welcome some 11 million guests yearly. There are spectacular malls or the small boutiques of Coconut Grove, and the waterfront Bayside Marketplace overlooking the city's Miamarina that offer an exceptional variety for shopping and dining. This is Miami at its tasteful best!

P. F. CHANG'S

17455 Biscayne Boulevard (305) 957-1966 Major Credit Cards
Lunch $8 Dinner $11

This China Bistro is unlike any oriental restaurant you have ever visited, for from the moment you enter P. F. Chang's, everything you see, from a huge mural to carved columns and statues, tells stories of Emperors, Gods and Guardians in ancient times. Even the menu offering cuisines of Canton, Szechwan, Hunan, Mongolia, Shanghai and unique specialties differs in its presentations. Chefs in an open kitchen create dishes with a delicious balance of taste, texture, color and aroma to satisfy all the senses. Every item is cooked to order, from warm duck salads or Chang's spicy Chicken to Chinese classics of Mongolian Beef and Mu Shu Pork. Nightly seafood specials like Kun Pao Scallops with peanuts and chili peppers, shrimp sauteed with chives, snow peas and wine or Paul's farm raised catfish fillets served with black bean sauce are sensational. Meals may be ordered and served "family style" for each guest to share and experience a multitude of exotic flavors and tastes. P. F. Chang's Bistro is a delicious blending of Chinese cuisine and culture with American hospitality.

Chef Roy's Favorite Chicken

1 lb chicken breasts
12 oz broccoli
1 tsp fresh ground ginger
1 oz scallions, chopped
1 tsp garlic, crushed
12 oz chicken stock
6 oz dark sauce
cornstarch
canola & sesame oil

Steam broccoli with chicken stock. Set aside & keep warm. Meanwhile cut chicken into large chunks & saute in hot canola oil until 3/4 done. Remove & add garlic, scallions, & ginger. Make dark sauce with soy sauce, sugar, oyster & mushroom sauce. Add to wok with chicken stock & reduce. Replace chicken & thicken with cornstarch & sesame oil. Cover plate with broccoli, top with chicken & spoon sauce over. Serves two.

HOUSTON'S

17355 Biscayne Blvd. (305) 947-2000 AE VISA MC
Lunch $8 Dinner $10

Houston's of North Miami Beach is built beside protected waters where patrons may watch manatee at play and private yachts cruising down the main stream of the Intracoastal Waterway. The beautiful view, however, is but one of the many attractions that make this one of the most popular restaurants along this section of Florida. They have designed a menu that is also main stream American cuisine which they prepare and serve better than almost anyone else at a very reasonable cost. Everything is made in house from daily signature soups and mammoth size salads to side dishes of iron skillet beans, couscous and desserts of warm nut brownies with champagne custard and homemade caramel. The kitchen is open and all may watch chefs barbecue chicken backyard style or grill fresh tuna steaks and prime filet mignon over hardwood coals. They serve aged prime rib and grind choice chuck for burgers or you can order one veggie style. Their beer, wines and ports are International in scope but the martini list is classic USA, typical of Houston's tried and true cuisine, service and ambiance.

Biscayne Bay Vodka Martini

3 oz Bleeder Vodka
1/2 oz Hiram Walker Triple Sec
cranberry juice
pineapple juice

Pour Bleeder vodka and Triple Sec into cocktail shaker with ice. Shake, do not stir and strain into chilled martini stem glass. Garnish with orange or mango slice.

Chocolate Martini

3-1/2 oz Chopin vodka
1/2 oz light Cream de Cocoa
Pour Chopin and Creme de Cocoa into cocktail shaker with ice and shake, do not stir. Meanwhile, rim martini glass with dark chocolate & chill. Pour martini into stem glass and garnish with shaved chocolate.

LOMBARDI'S

Bayside Marketplace 401 Biscayne Blvd. (305) 381-9580
Lunch $9 Dinner $12 Major Credit Cards

Alberto Lombardi began his career as a restaurateur working as a food server and bartender across most of Europe before sailing with Cunard Lines and moving to the States. He managed restaurants from coast to coast before opening his first Lombardi's in Dallas in 1977. Today Alberto has over half a dozen locations from Arizona to Florida, and dining at any one explains his success. He has perfected the cuisines of his mother country with authentic Northern Italian dishes served by an experienced and knowledgeable staff in impeccable surroundings. Lombardi's of Miami has an open kitchen where guests may watch chefs at work with the aroma of pizzas and homemade focaccia bread baking in a wood burning oven. Inside or on their open patio all patrons have beautiful views of Biscayne Bay and Miamarina while enjoying a lunch of Risotto Pescatore, Fettucine al Limone con Pollo at dinner or perhaps Gelati or Sorbetti at the unique Gelateria. Their SeaSide Bar is ideal for banquets and cocktail parties with music under the stars, making Lombardi's the hot spot in Miami for great food and fun.

Risotto Pescatore

8 medium shrimp
16 black mussels
8 Littleneck clams
4 oz calamari
4 oz scallops
3 cups lobster broth
1-1/2 lbs Arborio rice
4 oz tomatoes
4 tblsps chopped basil
4 tblsps chopped scallions
3 tblsps butter

Peel & clean shrimp & combine with mussels, scallops, clams & calamari cut into rings & tentacles. Cook in broth until shells open & almost done. Meanwhile cook rice for 30 minutes with butter, chopped onions & a little white wine. Add rice to seafood mixture with butter, scallions, tomatoes, salt & pepper to taste & cook to heat through. Serve in large bowls with seafood on top. Garnish with basil leaves. Serves four.

JOE'S STONE CRAB

227 Biscayne Street (305) 673-0365 Major Credit Cards
Lunch $25 Dinner $35 Closed Mid May to Mid Oct.

Joe's Stone Crab is without question the oldest, most historic and notable dining establishment in all of Florida. Its guests over decades have included Presidents, Royalty, and celebrities from Al Jolson to Al Capone. It began in 1913 when Joe Weiss sold fish sandwiches and fries at the only diner in the back-water town of Miami Beach. Back then Joe was also the first to discover that the stone crab was not only edible but incredibly delicious dipped in his special mustard sauce. From the beginning his stone crabs were a hit and lines formed with movie stars, artists, politicians, Damon Runyon characters and everyone who wanted to try a new taste sensation. Joe created a cole slaw, potato dishes and key lime pie that are still the favorites on their full menu today that lists steaks, chops, chicken and over two dozen seafood items. Joe's great grandson, Stephen Sawitz, now oversees a family tradition that covers two city blocks with restaurant, parking lots and even "Joe's Take-Away". Chef Amy Smith helps in hammering out tons of claws daily for hungry patrons who still line up to experience Joe's Stone Crab!!

Joe's Stone Crab Mustard Sauce

1 tblsp plus1/2 tsp dry Coleman's mustard
1 cup mayonnaise
2 tsps Worcestershire
1 tsp A-1 sauce
2 tblsps heavy cream
2 tblsps milk
salt

Place dry mustard in mixing bowl and add mayonnaise. Beat for 1 minute. Add Worcestershire sauce, A-1, cream and milk, and a pinch of salt and beat until mixture is well blended and creamy. If you like a little more mustard bite, whisk in 1/2 tsp more dry mustard until well blended. Cover and chill sauce. Serve in small cups with cooked and cracked stone crab claws. Makes about 1 cup sauce.

GREEN STREET CAFE

3110 Commodore Plaza (305) 444-0244 Major Cards
Brkfst $5 Lunch $7 Dinner $12

When you realize many local residents of Coconut Grove have been dining here daily for some 10 years, as other cafes in Coconut Grove come and go, then you know that the owner, chefs and staff at the Green Street Cafe are doing things very right. Sitting on one of the busiest intersections in town this is the perfect spot to see and be seen from breakfast to an after dinner brandy at midnight. Regardless of the time, there is something very special that keeps this placed packed yearly. It may start with French owner, Sylvano Bignon, whose charismatic smile, even while bussing tables, charms the toughest of tourists. It may be the staff following his lead with the friendliest service around. But perhaps it is the excellence and diversity of their cuisine listed on a six page menu with items from eggs with hot salsa to soups, salads, sandwiches, over a dozen pasta choices, lamburgers, blackened dolphin or veal Parisi. Add 100 great shooters, 10 coffee drinks, liqueurs and even Dom Perignon Pizza for just $125. If you're looking for great views, service and super food, just find the smart locals!

Sylvano's Grilled Chicken Salad

2 chicken breasts, boneless & skinned
Cajun seasoning
1 large tomato
1 cup yellow corn kernels
Romaine & iceburg lettuce
2 tblsps dijon mustard
2 tblsps olive oil
2 tblsps wine vinegar
1 egg
salt & pepper to taste

Sprinkle chicken breasts with Cajun seasoning & grill to desired doneness. Meanwhile, coarsely cut Romaine & iceburg lettuce, mix & mound on plates. Chop tomato & place over lettuce. Sprinkle with corn kernels, salt & pepper to taste. For vinaigrette, mix egg, dijon mustard, olive oil & vinegar, blend & pour over salad. Thinly slice chicken breasts & arrange on top. Serves two.

CAFE MED

Coco Walk 3015 Grand Avenue (305) 443-1770 Major Credit Cards
Lunch $8 Dinner $12

It is the only restaurant in the bustling Coco Walk complex that provides outside dining on the patio. And it is the only one with a menu printed in Italian with English subtitles, which suggests the cuisine is as authentic as it gets, unless you visit the same Cafe Med in Milan or New York. Owner Roberto Ruggie has designed his restaurants worldwide to feature classic Mediterranean dishes prepared and served in the manner and style so successful in the bistros and cafes of Europe. Dining here under palms and umbrellas or inside with brick archways and wooden beams makes Cafe Med in Coconut Grove a culinary trip to the Old Country. But it is really the cuisine created in an open kitchen like Ravioli di Ricotta, Lasagne alla Bolognese or the Salmone Grigliato that makes dining at this Cafe Med so popular. Everything is made in-house, from pasta and soups served in fresh bread bowls, to their Pizza Focaccine and homemade Tiramisu. There is a beautiful bar inside to enjoy a fine Italian wine or Cappuccino and another on the patio for lunching and watching a passing parade of visitors to this unique Italian Cafe Med.

Filet Mignon with Julienned Potatoes & Broiled Tomatoes

2 12 oz filet mignon
8 oz beef stock
4 oz red wine
2 tblsps butter
3 tomatoes
1 red onion
4 tblsps parmesan cheese
1 lb julienned potatoes

Lightly saute filets in butter on both sides until desired doneness. Remove, add beef stock reduced to pure beef base. Add red wine & butter slowly to desired taste. Meanwhile, slice tomatoes in half, scoop out centers & mix with 2 eggs, cheese & chopped red onion. Fill tomatoes with mixture & broil 5 minutes. Deep fry potatoes till golden & puffy. Arrange filets on plates with tomatoes, top with potatoes & spoon sauce around. Serves two.

LA FONTAINE

3390 Mary Street (305) 447-0553 Major Credit Cards
Lunch $7 Dinner $16

After years of renaissance with trendy new shops, cafes and hotels, visitors to Coconut Grove can finally enjoy genuine French provencale cuisine in the newly opened La Fontaine at the Streets of Mayfair's promenade. The decor is of a charming French country bistro with colorful banquettes and pastel chairs inside and marble cafe tables with wood benches on the outdoor fountain courtyard. It is the ideal setting for family and friends to enjoy a variety of traditional French staples from cassoulet, crepes, soup and salads to seafood, meats or pasta.

The Poulet Roti, Salimon au beurre blanc or Filet Mignon Sauce Bernaise simply prepared will satisfy any discriminating gourmet. The restaurant also includes a pastry shop filled with elegant cakes and parfaits and a delightful array of desserts as well as pates, and a selection of cheeses not found in typical markets. Along with a fine wine list of some 110 labels, a chef from Paris and world class cuisine, their most remarkable asset may well be proprietor Craig Liman, a 26 year old with a genius for designing restaurants and menus as delightful as his La Fontaine!

La Fontaine Poulet Roti

1 roasting chicken
olive oil
1 celery stalk
1 carrot
1 medium onion
fresh chopped thyme
fresh chopped rosemary
fresh oregano
demi glace
1/2 cup fresh cranberies
salt & pepper to taste

Fill chicken cavity with chopped celery, carrot & onion. Brush skin with olive oil & season with herbs, salt & pepper to taste. Marinate for 10 hours. Slowly roast in 350° oven until crispy & done. Remove chicken, add demi glace, herbs, cranberries and a little water to pan juice & reduce. Pour sauce on plates, top with cut pieces of chicken & garnish with rosemary & parsley. Serves two.

NEWS CAFE

2901 Florida Avenue 305-774-News Major Credit Cards
Bkfrst $5 Lunch $7 Dinner $9

The News Cafe in Coconut Grove and in South Beach, Miami are the only places you can pick up a French newspaper or classic paperback, order a cappuccino with Kahlua and enjoy the scenery from a European style sidewalk bistro. With a wide selection of international papers, books, cards and CD's, their Store also features an exclusive line of clothing, accessories and fine cigars for fun shopping between breakfast, lunch or dinner at the adjacent Cafe. Open 24 hours a day, their menu offers everything from bagels and blintzes for breakfast to a grilled salmon or N.Y. steak for dinner. Eggs and omelettes, over a dozen salads including Tabouli, Greek and Israeli, paté with brie, pastas and pizzas and every conceivable sandwich are just part of an incredible selection served in a casual, jazzy atmosphere. Their lists of beer and wine, single malt scotch, cognac and brandy are also extensive as well as desserts of cakes, pies, pastries and the ultimate chocolate fondue with strawberries and champagne for two. In fact, for reading, shopping, music, smoking, drinking and dining, News Cafe is the place to be!

Cold Poached Salmon with Herb Dressing

2 7 oz salmon fillets
1 cucumber
1 tomato
watercress
1 lemon
olive oil
herb dressing

Steam salmon fillets in 2" pan for 7 minutes. Remove, cover & refrigerate for one hour. For herb dressing: In a food processor, blend 1/4 cup each of watercress, parsley and tarragon, 1 oz spinach, 1 green onion, 3 egg yolks, 1 oz lemon juice, 1/3 cup yogurt, salt & pepper to taste. Slowly add 1 cup vegetable oil & blend to a mayonnaise consistency. Top salmon with herb dressing. Add diced tomatoes, cucumbers, watercress & mist with olive oil & lemon. Serves two.

SCOTTY'S LANDING

3385 Pan American Drive (305) 854-2626 VISA MC
Lunch $6 Dinner $8

It is understandable why local Groveites and boaters at Dinner Key Marina would like to keep their favorite waterside bar and grill a secret, for on balmy days and nights, Scotty's Landing is packed with lunch and dinner patrons enjoying frosty cold beers, platters of crispy cracked conch and gorgeous views of Biscayne Bay at sunset. It is as close to a barefoot Caribbean bistro as it gets in Florida with nautical memorabilia on the walls and umbrella shaded tables filling an open deck. The menu is typical of island fare featuring fresh grilled dolphin, spicy seafood chowder, crabcakes and even baby back ribs and steaks. Owner Scotty Wessel with his wife, Kate have recreated their favorite island haunts with casual waterfront dining and cuisine that attracts the cruising sailors as well as the commissioners of City Hall just a block away. It is not unusual to find Miami's City fathers holding unofficial meetings while munching on conch fritters and sipping cold brews on fresh air decks with awesome views of sailboats in the harbor. To enjoy casual waterfront dining away from cookie cutter franchises, sail to Scotty's Landing!

Lizzie's Bahamian Cracked Conch

1 lb conch meat
Juice of two limes
1 tblsp garlic powder
1 tsp Old Bay seasoning
2 eggs
flour
vegetable oil

Pound conch meat with mallet until soft and tender. Marinate in lime juice, garlic powder and Old Bay Seasoning for one hour. Cut conch meat into bite size pieces. Beat eggs into a batter. Dip conch pieces into batter and dredge in flour. Pan fry conch in hot vegetable oil for 3 to 4 minutes until brown and crispy. Drain and serve on lettuce bed with homemade french fries and cocktail sauce. Garnish with lime wedges. Serves two.

INDEX

ORDERING INFORMATION

These colorful companion guides featuring the best restaurants and cuisines from the Chesapeake Bay to the Caribbean Islands make the ideal gift for cruising yachtsmen, cooks and the traveling gourmet.

LEEWARD ISLANDS
A selection of the best dining from luxury resorts of Anguilla & Antigua, the French bistros of St. Martin & St. Barts to the plantations of St. Kitts & Nevis are captured in pictures & words.

PUERTO RICO
The variety of restaurants on this beautiful island, from elegant hotels of San Juan to remote mountain chalets & coastal resorts, are featured in this diner's guide with recipes from some of the Caribbeans finest chefs.

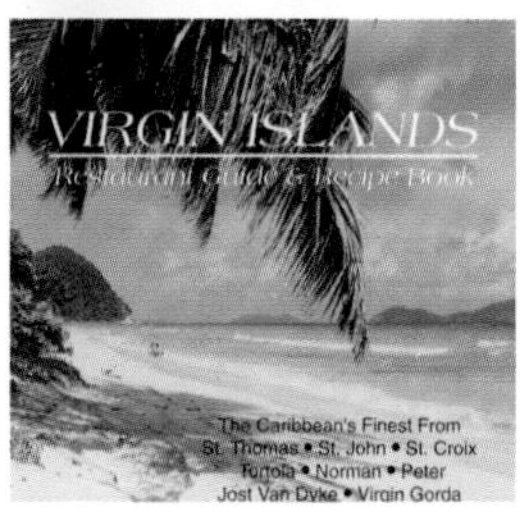

VIRGIN ISLANDS
Take a culinary cruise through the U.S. & British Virgins in this dining guide that features the best from St. Thomas, St. Croix & St. John to Tortola, Virgin Gorda & Jost Van Dyke..its a delicious sailing paradise.

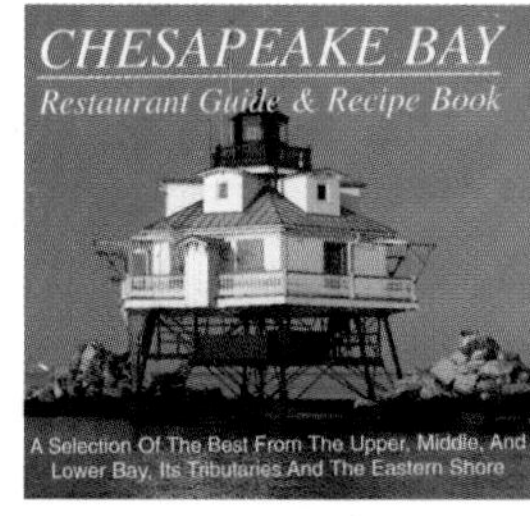

CHESAPEAKE BAY
Restaurants lining the shores and tributaries of this bountiful Bay offer a variety of fresh seafood, poultry, meats and game. The best from Baltimore to Virginia Beach are featured in this must guide for boaters and gourmets.

To order copies of these informative guides, contact any of the distribution services listed below. For information regarding the authors and their publication write Susan & Charles Eanes % Espichel Enterprises, 1401 Connecticut Ave, Glen Allen, Virginia, 23060 or by e-mail at editor@dineashore.com Visit their Website at www.dineashore.com [or at] http://www.icw-net.com

Phone & Credit Card Orders
Cruising Guide Publications
P.O. Box 1017
Dunedin, FL. 34697-1017
1-800-330-9542

For Booksellers
Douglas Charles Press
7 Adamsdale Road
North Attleboro, MA. 02760
(508) 761-7721

For Maritime Outlets
Robert Hale & Co.
1803 132th Ave. N.E. S #4
Bellvue, Wash. 98005
1-800-733-5330